Social Media

Marketing Handbook for

Soulful Entrepreneurs

The Complete Guide To Creating A Soulful and

Successful Social Media Strategy

Beckie Coupe

Contents

Why You Should Read This Book

- Are you stuck in a rut with social media - struggling to get started or unsure what to do next and how to actually get results from your efforts?

- Do you find that something works OK for a while but then all of a sudden you're back to square one and you have no idea why?

- Are you overwhelmed with all the advice and information that is thrown your way and struggling to sort the good from the bad?

- Do some of the strategies, tricks and hacks that you hear about feel 'off' to you and the thought of implementing them makes you feel completely uncomfortable?

If you answered 'yes' to any of those questions, then *Social Media Marketing Handbook for Soulful Entrepreneurs* is for you!

This book will guide you through the process of creating a successful social media marketing strategy that helps you to build the business of your dreams in a way that feels utterly soulful and brimming with integrity.

What you learn in the pages that follow will empower you to take control of your social media marketing, learn to enjoy the process and embrace connecting with your dream clients on this far-reaching medium.

You will banish the stress and the overwhelm that's so often associated with using social media for business and discover how to keep your sanity intact and even have fun with it!

So grab your copy of this book right now and make sure you have your notebook and pen at the ready because the ideas are going to start flowing for you right from the very first chapter!

Foreword

It's an absolute honour to be asked to write this foreword for Beckie's first book.

As you leaf through the pages of this book and open your mind to the possibility that social media has to offer you then Beckie will lead you by the hand and make the seemingly senseless world of social media a whole host less daunting.

We are super privileged to live in a digital age where we have the power to connect with the world at our fingertips and I'm super grateful for the opportunities that it affords to me when it comes to building my business. The thing is, though, that social media can often feel like the rabbit hole in Alice in Wonderland. Initially it feels like a scary prospect to enter the realms of worldwide connection, then you seem to fall into a quandary about what you should be doing and how you should be doing it and, left to its own devices, you can end up completely consumed by social media.

Social media is a very powerful part of your marketing mix and what Beckie is so good at doing is bringing absolute sense and a practical guide to using these medium of connection. It's not about you broadcasting out there to your audience and shouting the loudest. It's about making connections, connections that you can nurture and grow and connections to whom you offer a genuine interest, help and support.

Beckie has been an absolute integral part of helping me to develop my social media strategy and within the pages of this book she's going to open your mind to the potential and possibility that social media has for you too.

Beckie's guidance will change the way you think about your social media, it will open the doors to brand, spanking new opportunity for you and it'll ultimately help you to make more money ~ and what's not to love about that?

You're totally in safe hands here.

Grab a notebook because I reckon the ideas are going to fly.

Big Love,

Emma Holmes, Rebels & Rockstars

Why Soulful Social Media?

I am delighted that you have picked up this book and taken the first step towards creating a social media strategy that is going to help you to build and grow the business of your dreams!

So often social media is labelled as something that we, as business owners, 'should' be doing. We see the popularity of social media across almost all aspects of our society and the immense power it holds to connect people and spread information, and with that we feel the pressure to be using social media both personally and to get our businesses out into the world. However, over the past decade that I've spent working with businesses and helping them harness the power of social media, I've witnessed how the pressure to be present on social media leads many entrepreneurs to be frozen between expectation and taking positive and productive action to use social media to their advantage.

My hope is that as you read through the pages of this book social media becomes less of a 'should' and more of a would, could and will. No matter what stage you are at on your journey in business and in the world of social media I want you to feel empowered to make it your own. To map your own journey and follow that path towards creating a business and a lifestyle that you absolutely love and adore. And that latter part is as important to me, and I hope to you too, as the success of your business is. Whatever label you want to give yourself, business owner, self-employed, entrepreneur, your business is as much a part of you as every other aspect of your life. You will live, eat and sleep it so it really should be something that lights you up and fills you with passion and enthusiasm. Every aspect of your business should support you on your journey. If there is any element that is keeping you up at night with worry or which you dread working on then something is not working as it should and it's time to change it.

When it comes to social media, there are two sides to that coin.

The first is you need to find a way to manage your social media that empowers you to share your message with the world. If you decide to delegate any or all of your social media marketing that's absolutely fine but you will, nevertheless, be the captain of your own ship and your vision must always be the driving force behind your marketing.

Secondly, your social media marketing should be working in your favour to attract your ideal, best-fit clients. We'll talk about the concept of 'ideal clients' and what it means throughout this book but I want you to have it in mind right from the beginning. Your ideal clients are those people who absolutely love what you offer, they are the ones who will benefit most from your product or service and, in turn, you will love working with them and they will often prove to be the most profitable source of business. When you hone your social media marketing in on those ideal clients you will see results that far exceed what can be achieved when you try to be all things to all people. Social media will then be supporting you in creating a business <u>and</u> a lifestyle you love. If you're kept up at night because your customers never seem to be satisfied, they grumble about the price and they don't seem to value what you do for them then the chances are, you are attracting the wrong people.

I've been in that position and I can honestly say that when I re-assessed my marketing strategy and, for the first time, truly understood who I should be marketing to and serving, it transformed my business. I was able to create a community who recognise the value in what I do for them. We share an excitement to work together and seeing the difference that I can help make to their world is what gets me up in the morning! It's why I'm in business.

There are lots of different ways you can make money but doing what you love and working with the people you are passionate about helping has got to be the best way, hasn't it?

You Will Get Out What You Put In

As is the case with most things in life, you will get out of social media what you put into it. I'm not necessarily talking here about the time or money you invest into social media, although of course those are important factors, but rather I'm referring specifically to the energy you invest in it.

There is something really special about social media that means the energy you or your team put into it has a direct impact on the outcomes you experience.

Perhaps that seems a little wishy-washy but think of it this way; social media, more so than any other marketing medium, is about the connections you make with other people and the relationships you build. It is a direct line between your business and your customers. It is not about broadcasting a message from a distance; its very power lies in the fact that it brings you and your customers together to form a community. The conversation becomes two-way – or, even three-way, four-way and more - as you draw more people into the fold.

Your energy has an impact on all of the relationships in your life. If you are tired then you might find yourself being grumpy with other people and that leads to negative outcomes. If you're unwell then you may not feel that you have a lot to offer to other people at that moment and you retreat into yourself. Whilst the outcome may not be negative, as such, you may feel that your relationships stagnate during that time and you have less positive experiences together. The same is true on social media.

Gone are the days when you could hide behind a logo and create a public persona for your business that was professional but impersonal. People want and expect to see the person or people behind the brand. As businesses have become more and more active on social media and we, as consumers, have become more surrounded by marketing messages and advertising, scepticism has risen. We don't want to feel that we are being sold to, yet again, by a nameless, faceless corporation. What most people are lacking and striving for are meaningful connections in their lives, not just with friends and family but with businesses and organisations as well.

That means the people behind your brand are its driving force. Whether you have a team of 100 or you're working solo, your energy will shape your message and its outcomes.

If you're paying lip-service to social media and posting whatever you can find just to be present then you won't see much back in return or, what you do get back will not be ideal. It certainly won't help you create a business that you adore. If you invest your time and energy into lovingly crafting content that resonates with your ideal client then the business that you attract will allow you to thrive.

Why Soulful Social Media?

This is where the concept of soulful social media comes in, and throughout the pages of this book I am going to show you how to create a social media strategy that is utterly soulful, successful and sustainable.

You may have come across strategies and teachings in the past that don’t sit quite right with you. They make you feel uncomfortable, they don't resonate with you or your crowd and, therefore, don't get the results you hope for.

Social media with soul offers a different way of doing business. It...

- allows everything that makes you and your business unique and special to shine through
- doesn’t feel forced, pushy, unrelenting or insincere
- doesn’t sap away your time and energy
- sets you apart from the masses, without you feeling the need to compete with others
- is sustainable and effective - no one-hit wonders or ‘hacks’

- resonates with the right people at the right time
- enables you to serve your mission

It is not about impressing people - it's about impacting them.

It is about building your business with integrity, ditching the hustle, staying true to yourself and your values and having fun in the process.

If that leaves you feeling excited to get started then dive on in to the rest of this book and start creating your very own soulful social media strategy.

Chapter 1 – Strategy

One of the things I love most about social media is that anyone can jump in and put their business out there for the world to see. Gone are the days of having to find money for websites, leaflets and advertising before you could even get started with marketing your business. Now you can hop over to your chosen social media platform and dive straight in.

But, just imagine… you've been sat with this sparkly new business idea and you cannot wait to shout about it from the rooftops. You set up your social media platforms and pages and pop a few posts on. And then… nothing! You can practically hear the tumbleweeds rolling by and you find yourself stalling before you've even got started.

The support of friends and family can go a long way at this early stage. By its very nature, social media is the ideal place for spreading messages by word of mouth. You might find that your friends and family are more than happy to follow you, share in your excitement and some of them may even become your very first customers.

There is absolutely nothing wrong with tapping into your own network in the early days of building your business. In fact, that's exactly how I got started! The very first thing I did, before I 'officially' launched Infinity, was to share my plans with my friends, family and, most importantly, people I had worked with in the past. Not only did this help me secure my first few clients, but it also helped me to build up a small base of social media followers which gave me a starting point to spring forward from.

Do be careful about who you invite to follow your business, however, and only reach out to those people who you know will be supportive. It's amazing how a flippant comment about a Facebook post, even if it's not inherently negative, can trigger a serious case of the wobbles. If you're worried about what your friends are going to think every time you post something on social media, then you'll end up diluting your message. In fact, I find this is one of the common reasons people avoid recording videos in particular!

Moving Beyond Friends and Family

You might find in the early days that wins and milestones are aplenty – a few people start liking your posts, you hit your first 100 followers, you let out a little cheer when your first enquiry or sale rolls in. It's an exciting time and, no doubt, you're brimming with enthusiasm and excitement, but what happens if all that engagement begins to stagnate or dwindle?

With the best will in the world, it's safe to say that pretty much everyone hits this stumbling block at some point, and it will probably happen more than once. For some, it can happen within days of setting up their social media pages.

So, no matter how big or small your crowd is to start with, at some point you will recognise that it is time to move beyond your immediate network and word of mouth marketing.

The sooner you start to build a crowd of followers who adore your content and jump at the chance to buy from you, the sooner you will create a soulful, sustainable and strong social media strategy.

Even if you haven't drawn on your existing network and you've been lucky enough to build a crowd of followers from the ground up, without a strategy it can be difficult to maintain the momentum. The key is to take action before things begin to plateau.

Always Put Your Followers First

We'll talk a lot more about attracting a crowd of your biggest fans in a later chapter, but for now, I just want to point to them as being the focal point of your soulful social media strategy.

Beyond business growth, keeping your crowd at the centre of everything you do - not just on social media but in all aspects of your marketing - means that those peaks and troughs of enthusiasm will be less extreme. You will always have an anchor that you can pull yourself back towards if ever you feel lost.

Just as your business will evolve over time, so will your social media strategy.

Every time you learn something new about your crowd or you better understand what makes them tick, you will strengthen your anchor. Likewise, every time you learn more about a platform you're using, or you use analytics to put an element of your strategy to the test, you will gain more clarity, direction and purpose.

A Sustainable Strategy Brings Long-Term Benefits

Acknowledging that this is a process of evolution, and not a task that you complete once and review every so often, if at all, makes for a more sustainable and successful strategy.

Dipping in and out of your social media strategy, rather than using it to guide you each and every day, makes for a bumpy rollercoaster ride! You will have periods of immense action where your rollercoaster cart climbs high into the sky, times of inaction where progress plateaus and your cart rolls steadily along the track, and even periods of decline where engagement or sales start to drop off and you feel like you're rolling backwards.

Slow and Steady Wins the Race.

Yes, it's great to dedicate specific times for planning and strategising, but there should never be a day goes by where you are not reflecting on your social media activity and how it is performing. There will still be some ups and downs along the way, just as there is in all areas of business, but placing yourself firmly in the driving seat will go a long way towards smoothing out your journey.

What's more, it makes the whole process of tweaking and improving your social media strategy so much easier.

Think of it this way, if you were to conduct a scientific experiment you would usually test one variable against another. You would take great care to ensure that every other variable remained the same so that you could, as far as possible, identify cause and effect.

The same goes for your social media strategy. To put it simply, a social media strategy is about doing more of what works and less of what doesn't. If you implement lots of different changes at the same time it becomes impossible to pinpoint what's working and what isn't. You might gain short-term results, but you have no light to illuminate your long- term strategy.

Tuning into your strategy on a day-to-day basis and being patient with progress is the best route to success in the long-term.

Think Strategy First, Excitement Second

The last thing I'd ever want to do is to kill your enthusiasm, but it is important to channel your energy and excitement into strategic action. That's not to say that everything you do has to be micro-planned and your social media strategy doesn't have to be rigid and stuff, in fact it shouldn't be. It mores about ensuring that there is a purpose behind everything you do.

As you read through this book, I want you to take each point you learn and consider where it fits within your strategy. Is it something you can implement straightaway? Or is it an action you need to follow up further down the line? Is there something you need to put in place first before you can follow up on the next action?

I absolutely want you to be buzzing with enthusiasm and ideas by the time you've finished reading, but I'm here to prep you and guide you towards social media success over the coming weeks, months, and even years - not just today.

Know What You Want To Achieve

In order to put each element of your strategy to the test, we need to have an idea of what success on social media looks like. This is something to think about before we move on to considering what your strategy is going to look like.

If your goal on social media is to achieve internet fame and attention then you will probably measure success based on the size of your audience, how much engagement your posts receive and the opportunities for publicity which you attract.

By contrast, if you're using social media to help you achieve grow your business, both in terms of financial sales and customer base, then those metrics are only worth measuring if they have an underlying benefit to your business. In other words, attention for attention's sake is meaningless unless that is your overall goal.

Think About Your Business Objectives

With that in mind, the starting point of your social media strategy should be your overall business objectives. What are your reasons for using social media? What are you hoping to achieve?

Your answers to these questions will, of course, be unique to your business but may include; increased brand awareness, more traffic to your website, more enquiries generated, more sales secured, credibility as an expert in your field and to grow your professional network. You can have more than one objective for your social media marketing, and specific goals may vary on different platforms.

'To grow my business' isn't specific enough because it gives you no check-in point; it can leave you scratching your head, not knowing whether you're getting things right or wrong and unsure how to make progress.

A vague objective like this can also lead to missed opportunities. I come across this often in the case of Twitter – the #1 platform people tell me they simply don't see the point of. When I dig deeper to understand why people can't see the point of Twitter, it's often because their sole social media objective is to grow their business and, if Twitter isn't directly generating enquiries or sales for them, that's justification to write it off. In actual fact, Twitter could be fantastic for driving traffic to your website, attracting subscribers to your email list and even presenting PR opportunities that will help you raise your profile and enhance your credibility. It's not always about direct sales. There are other goals that can help you to achieve that overall vision for your business.

Whatever stage you're at on your social media journey right now, pause and get clear on your objectives. If your starting point is business growth then that is absolutely fine, but break it down from there into objectives that will contribute to your overall growth. For now, we're not setting specific goals or targets but, instead, we're getting crystal clear on the overall objectives of your strategy.

Having these objectives in place will give you a benchmark for evaluating your strategy, which we'll talk about in more detail in Chapter 8, in terms of being clear on what success looks like and knowing where there is room for improvement. For example, if one of your Facebook posts gets thousands of likes it would be tempting to deem this post a success. But if your aim is to spark conversation so that you can create meaningful connections with your followers and, in turn, nurture them into becoming paying customers, a post with thousands of likes but few comments indicates room for improvement. Rather than chalking up a successful post and leaving it at that, recognising that the post could be improved to get you closer to achieving your objective is going to be of much more benefit to your business. This is the point where you can start asking meaningful questions; why didn't this post receive many comments? Am I reaching the right people? Was there something in the content that made people feel unable or unwilling to comment? What can I do next time to encourage more comments?

You've now got the backbone of a social media strategy that will deliver real business benefits and continue to evolve with ease.

So we've talked about:

- strategy as an abstract
- as an ever-evolving plan that will guide your activity on social media
- and we've discussed what success looks like

I also want you to keep in mind that your objectives and what you view as success will change as you make progress. As entrepreneurs we have a habit of moving the goal posts. Each time you achieve a goal or you come close to it you will, more than likely, set a new goal and your idea of success will shift, even if you're not aware of it. It's easy to get disheartened as 'success' always seems to be just out of reach but, instead, I want you to keep checking in with how far you've come, what you've achieved and be aware of when you've moved the goal posts as this will push you to keep growing and moving forward.

Creating A Social Media Strategy

The answer is, there is no one style or form of strategy that will work for everyone. It will very much depend on the nature of your business and, importantly, on your own personal working style.

For some people, a Word document works perfectly, for others it may be a spreadsheet, or a diagram or even a Trello board (my personal favourite). The important thing is that whatever document or layout you choose, it is structured in a way that can be easily adapted and evolved. Your strategy should be a working document; if it feels too rigid then you will be reluctant to change it and it's likely to become one of those things you pour time and energy into once, only to file and forget about.

Bear in mind that you don't have to have all the answers when you first lay out your social media strategy. For example, one of the questions that I ask clients in my 1-2-1 strategy sessions is 'who else does your ideal client follow on social media?' This is the point most people start doing a lot of umming and ahhing because, either, they've never thought about it or they don't know how to find the answer out.

So when I help them to put together their social media strategy this will be highlighted as an action point for them to go away and follow up. Approaching it this way means that you don't have to wait until you have all the answers before creating your strategy (and, in all honesty, you will never have all the answers) and it also means your strategy has become a useful document which provokes action right from the get go.

As you tick things off your action list, you then need to go back into your strategy and update the plan. With the example of who else your ideal clients follow, you would add this information to your strategy once you've done your research, and then, and this is equally as important, you should ask yourself, what next?

What Comes Next?

In fact, **what next?** should be a question that's always on your lips. It's this simple question that will keep your strategy moving forward.

Whilst your strategy will evolve on a day-to-day basis, there will also be times when the answer to 'what next' will be to up-level. We're going to talk about up-levelling in more depth in Chapter 8 but, for now, I want to introduce you to the idea that social media isn't the kind of business project that can be wrapped up neatly and ticked off your to-do list. There will be times when you feel comfortable with your social media strategy and you're tempted to think, 'I just need to keep doing what I'm doing and everything will keep ticking over.' But it won't be like this all of the time. It would be nice if that were the case, wouldn't it?

By all means you could take this approach, but if you don't continue to be pro-active then your social media strategy will eventually stagnate. Your business and your crowd will continue to evolve whilst your social media presence stands still, which makes stagnation almost inevitable. What's more, the very nature of social media means that it's constantly changing. Strategies that are working right now may not work in quite the same way in a few months' time. New features will be released, algorithms will change, trends will shift and with it, your strategy must evolve too.

That's not to say that achieving success on social media has to be a daunting task, only that it requires you to adapt and be willing to ask, 'what next?'. In fact, the very reason I've written this book is because I want to provide you with a check-in point and a light to illuminate your path at every turn, as much as I want to give you a solid starting point for your social media strategy.

Bringing It All Together

So let's just have a quick recap on what you've learnt in this first chapter. You now know what a social media strategy is and why it's so important to the longevity of your business (and success on social media). You know all about sustainability, how to start creating a social media strategy and how to make the best possible use of it in your business. I've also introduced you to the all-important question – what next? – which is going to prepare you for evolving and up-levelling your strategy.

As you start to bring together your social media strategy, here are the core elements that I recommend you include. The following chapters will help you answer all of these key points.

- Objectives
- Key messages
- Tone of voice
- Target audience and ideal clients
- Which social media platforms you're going to use
- Content ideas
- Weekly schedule

So with the strategy foundation now in place, let's get ready for the next chapter: 'Your Clients Are The Heart Of Your Social Media'.

Chapter 2 – Your Clients Are The Heart Of Your Social Media

When you place your customers at the heart of your marketing you pave the way for your success.

Nowhere is this truer than on social media. The clue is in the name; **social** media. I know that this may seem like an obvious point to make when you see it written in black and white, but it is so easy to overlook the social element when you're focused on achieving marketing goals. Many businesses fall into the trap of broadcasting what they have to offer to potential customers, and forget to be social and forge genuine connections.

The power of social media lies in its ability to bring people together.

It can connect us with our customers, and potential customers, in a way that was not previously possible.

Look back ten years or so, and marketing was all about broadcasting your message. Perhaps you would have placed an advert in a newspaper, run an ad on the radio or showcased your products and services on your website. All of these channels were fantastic for spreading the word but what they didn't facilitate was an open dialogue between your business and your audience. Of course, you would carefully craft a message that you hoped would resonate with potential customers but the opportunities to actually converse with them and get instant feedback were limited.

Social Media Has Changed the Game.

It brings us closer to our audience than we have ever been before. Social media enables us to understand them on a more intimate level. It allows us to build meaningful relationships them, and that is what makes it such an extraordinarily powerful marketing tool.

In fact, this is the reason I prefer to think of them as a crowd rather than an audience, as our job is not to perform for them but to engage with them.

So, how can you leverage social media in an utterly soulful way to grow your business?

Let Your Crowd Become Your Anchor

Your customers should be at the heart of everything that you do on social media and beyond. It is when you lose sight of your customers' wants and needs that you find yourself drifting off to sea and hopelessly broadcasting your sales messages from afar.

Take a moment to picture your business as a boat out in the ocean. There are lots of other boats sailing around you, all of them are different sizes and are travelling to different destinations. Without your map and compass you will get lost on your journey. I'm going to equip you with your map and compass in the next chapter but, even more dangerous than sailing without a map, is sailing without an anchor. You may know the place you are trying to reach but if you don't have an anchor then you will end up floating off to sea and having to spend your precious time and resources on finding your way again.

Your crowd is your anchor

There will be times when you feel lost at sea with social media. It's at these times that you need to drop the anchor and check your compass. Allow your understanding of your crowd to steady your ship so that you can get your bearings and get back on course. Over time, as you learn more about your crowd, your anchor will become even stronger and the occasions when you feel lost will be less frequent, although it may still happen from time to time.

Focus On Your Ideal Clients

Before you can install the anchor on your ship, you need to know who is actually in your crowd. Your first answer is likely to be 'potential customers, of course!' but it's important that we start to narrow that down.

This is the point where many people get stuck. I'm going to ask you to narrow your target market right down and be as specific as possible about who is going to buy your products or services. It may feel uncomfortable at first, as you want to reach as many people as possible and serve anyone and everyone who could possibly benefit from what you have to offer. It's natural to feel that way and there is nothing wrong with the logic, but if you try to market to everyone you will connect with no-one.

This is true for all aspects of your marketing, but particularly so on social media. We've discussed how social media is all about creating connections and forming meaningful relationships so the same social norms apply as in 'real' life. To put it bluntly, you won't be everyone's cup of tea, and nor will everyone be yours. And that's absolutely fine!

If you try to appeal to an audience that is too broad and diverse then you will find that your message becomes diluted. It is impossible to please a whole spectrum of people. You won't truly understand and connect with those people who would snap your hand off at the opportunity to buy from you because your focus is too wide. You may worry about putting some people off, and therefore hold back on a message that would really resonate with those who are willing to buy. What's more, you may well attract customers who are not a good fit for you and your business. You will come across grumblers who don't value your service, who always want to barter on price and who will never be wholly satisfied with what you deliver, no matter how fantastic it may be.

For example, one of the services that I offer is social media management. In theory, any business that wants to have a presence on social media could benefit from the service that I provide. However, there are business owners who simply want social media 'off their desk', they want someone to take care of it with minimal involvement from their side but they still want to see fantastic results. This isn't ideal for me because I know that I won't be able to get the best possible results for their business without open and continued communication and input from the client. Their satisfaction and my own job satisfaction comes from achieving fantastic results that help their business to grow so this scenario wouldn't be ideal. What's more, they may not place a great deal of value on social media marketing in the first place; they believe that they 'should' be there but they're not fully invested in it. Unfortunately, that means that, no matter what I do, they may never be satisfied and with the service or with the cost.

It is for these reasons that focusing on your **ideal** clients will make your marketing more efficient and effective, your business more profitable, and it will keep your love for your business intact. After all, there's nothing more demoralising than working with clients who don't value what you do, is there?

Who Are Your Ideal Clients?

Another reason why the concept of ideal clients becomes a sticking point for many people is because they get hung up on pinning down details that aren't actually important.

You may have heard marketing gurus talk about creating a customer profile or avatar. These sorts of exercises often involve giving your 'ideal client' a name, describing what he or she looks like, even cutting out pictures from magazines to represent them visually. The problem here is that you fall into the trap of trying to be too specific. It's a delicate balance and narrowing your focus too much can be just as dangerous as being too broad. You will either end up creating a message that speaks to one individual (imaginary) person or staying stuck and taking no action whatsoever.

You only need to know the details which are going to help you form meaningful relationships with your crowd, so you need to create a filter that is relevant to your business.

You don't need to pin down where they live, unless it's relevant to the product or service you deliver. You needn't narrow down a specific age range, unless doing so helps you to create a more powerful proposition. You only need to know what your ideal clients have for breakfast if it links back to the message you want to share with them.

Your filter, therefore, is based on what's important to your business and what's important to your crowd.

What Are The Important Questions To Consider?

There is nothing worse than starting a task with a blank piece of paper! If you don't know what questions to ask, how can you possibly hope to find the answers?

The following questions are a starting point for you. As you become more familiar with your crowd and more comfortable with the concept of concentrating on your ideal clients, the way your understanding of them develops will become more fluid, but you can always refer back to these prompts and to your own notes any time you need to drop that anchor. I've also included an example in the bonus resources of the completed exercise, to give you an idea of how to approach the questions.

Who is Your Ideal Client?

This first question is about demographics; how old are they, where do they live, are they male or female, do they work in a specific occupation, and so on.

Remember, this information only matters if it is important to your business!

If your crowd includes both males and females that's absolutely fine but, equally, don't be afraid to narrow it down to a specific gender if it feels right to do so. Likewise, if age is irrelevant then you needn't answer, but if it is then remember that different age groups and generations will have varying interests and will respond to content in different ways.

What Are Your Ideal Clients Struggling With?

Often, the products or services that we provide as a business meet a certain need or solve a specific problem for our ideal clients. Your marketing should be less about 'selling' and more about communicating how you can meet that need or solve that problem, because that's what is really important to your customers.

What Do Your Ideal Clients Desire?

Your ideal clients' desires may link back to the problem or struggle that they have.

For example, if they are overweight then their struggles may include health issues, lack of confidence, not feeling like 'themselves' and perhaps even frustration with failed diets and exercise regimes in the past. Their desires, therefore, might include fitting into their clothes comfortably, feeling more confident in their own skin, improving their health and having more energy. They may also have some desires around how they achieve these outcomes. For example, perhaps they don't have much free time and therefore they want a solution that won't involve spending hours in the gym, or perhaps they don't want to do a lot of cooking so they want healthy meals to be delivered to them.

The more information you can gather about the wants and needs of your ideal clients and also about how they want those wants and needs to be met, the more effectively and persuasively you will be able to present your product or service to them on social media. You will be able to form bonds with your crowd that convert your followers into your biggest fans and best customers!

In this way, your understanding of your ideal clients will act as a filter for potential clients, as well as for your marketing message. Going back to the weight loss example, if you are a personal trainer in a gym setting and you are using social media to talk to people who don't want to or can't work out in a gym, then you are going to have an uphill battle trying to get those people to book sessions with you. Even if they do become customers, are they going to stick with it long enough to see results? Are they going to value your service? Are they going to grumble about how much they're paying you?

In the meantime, potential clients who would love the structure and discipline of working with a personal trainer in the gym may not be entirely convinced by your message if it has become diluted by your efforts to try and appeal to the other group as well or instead of them.

What Is Holding Your Ideal Clients Back From Purchasing?

Using your social media posts, and other marketing content, to speak directly to your ideal clients' struggles and desires will be enough to take some followers straight through to becoming paying customers. However, others may stand right at the precipice and never take that final step to become a customer. There are often barriers that hold people back from making a purchase, particularly for the first time, and your marketing has an important role to play in helping your customers to move past their barriers, which could include;

- Uncertainty about whether your product or service is going to meet their needs.
- A lack of trust in your company, which is not necessarily for any negative reason but could

be purely because they don't know enough about your business or offering.

- Bad experiences with other providers of a similar product or service in the past.
- Overwhelmed by choice, either from your business specifically or others on the market.
- They don't yet fully value the product or service enough to invest in it; that's not to say they never will, just that they don't comprehend its value completely yet.

There are lots of other reasons why people will connect and engage with you on social media but not feel ready to buy from you, and you can often find out why by listening to your customers. Every time someone asks you a question or enquires about your product or service they are giving you clues to their barriers.

Pay close attention to the conversations you have with your customers, both potential and existing, and start keeping notes. I have a lovely hardback notebook that has become my ideal client journal. Anytime I learn something about my ideal clients I note it down in my journal and any questions I get asked by potential clients get jotted down too. Having a notebook like this is how your anchor can take on physical form. Whether you're stuck for content ideas or you're unsure how to connect with your crowd, refer back to your notebook and, I promise, you will not stay stuck for long!

It's also really important that you continue to evolve your understanding of your ideal clients. This is not a 'do it once and file it away' kind of exercise. The more you connect with your ideal clients the more you will learn about them and you can feed that knowledge back into your marketing for a stronger and more successful strategy.

Where Do They Hang Out On Social Media?

Now that you are starting to get to know what makes your ideal clients tick, we need to know where they hang out on social media.

In Chapter 4 we'll take a closer look at different social media platforms and how you can make a decision about which to focus on, but for now I want you to consider where your ideal clients are spending their time online. This won't be the only deciding factor when you're selecting social media platforms, as we will go on to discuss, but it is, of course, important.

To some extent, this knowledge can be gleaned from your understanding of the social media platforms you're already familiar with. For example, you might already know that your ideal clients are hanging out on Facebook because they are talking to you there or you have seen them engaging with businesses similar to yours, but be wary of making assumptions. If you have existing clients, ask them which social media platforms they use; you might even be able to probe a little further and find out how they're using them. Remember, this is about them not you. If you discover that your crowd love using a certain platform but you're not familiar or comfortable with it then take action to get comfortable with it. Don't close the door on a potential opportunity to connect with your crowd on a platform that they love because you don't love it, although it certainly does go a long way if you can find the love for the platform too!

Who Do Your Ideal Clients Follow On Social Media?

This is the final piece of the puzzle when it comes to understanding your ideal clients and it will come in particularly handy when you are creating content for social media.

Having said that, you might find this a tricky question to answer at first. A brain dump is a great way to get started; just grab a sheet of paper and list all the other social media pages your ideal clients might follow. Think outside of the box – it's not an exercise in listing competitors but rather understanding the interests of your crowd and the type of content they love to engage with. So, you might think about the blogs they read, the magazines they like, the celebrities they follow, the podcasts they listen to, the television programmes they watch and so on.

If your existing clients are willing to open up to you about how they use social media, then this is a great question to ask them. You could also ask questions on your own social media, such as what's your favourite magazine? Which blogs do you love to read? Do you enjoy listening to podcasts?

Remember, you don't need to get hung up on nailing down a rigid customer 'avatar'. The individuals within your crowd are exactly that; unique individuals. Their specific interests will vary but we're looking to find common threads that you can use to draw them together.

Bringing It All Together

So, in this chapter we've talked about how important it is to focus your marketing on your ideal clients, how to profile your customers and what are the really important pieces of information to gather. In the following chapters we will explore this further and discuss how you can use the insight you gain about your ideal clients to inform the content you create and share.

Chapter 3 – Social Media with Purpose

As you lay the foundations of your social media strategy you will, ideally, be attentive to your overall objectives; using the goals you want to achieve as the starting point of your plan. I touched on the benefits of social media in Chapter 1, and explained how setting objectives can provide valuable touch points. The key to achieving soulful and sustainable success, however, is to use social media with purpose each and every day.

Big picture objectives can easily be forgotten about, just as business plans that were once prepared in earnest can soon find themselves filed away and forgotten about. If we remember that our social media strategy is our map to success, then it's clear that we will soon become lost if we stop referring to it.

If you've been 'winging it' on social media up until now, it's not too late for you to hit the pause button, craft your strategy and refocus your efforts. That's not to say that everything you've done up until this point needs to be cast aside, quite the opposite. Whatever has gone before will help to illuminate the path you take now. Spend some time reflecting on what you have been doing. Don't be afraid to call out things that have fallen short but, equally, do acknowledge what has or is working for your business on social media.

Connecting Social Media To Your Business Mission

Whether you're aware of it or not, as an entrepreneur you are on a mission.

Large corporate companies often have a mission statement that is painstakingly crafted and communicated across an entire organisation. The mission statement will usually summarise the business's purpose, the market it serves, its vision for the future and the values it operates by.

As an entrepreneur and business owner you may not have ever considered your mission in such a formal way, but you will likely know why you created your business, what its purpose is, who it serves and the values you stand by. This is the cornerstone of your business, a benchmark against which you can make strategic decisions, including decisions about your social media marketing.

Take some time now to write down your mission. It doesn't have to be lengthy and try not to overthink it; you already have the answers, it's just a case of bringing them forth. A few short sentences that clarify your purpose, who you serve, and your values is all that's needed. Keep your mission somewhere that will serve as a constant reminder, whether it be pinned to your office wall or set as the background on your desktop.

You can now connect your social media activity to your mission. Your mission will influence your decisions on everything from the content that you share to the tone that you use and the way that you build relationships with your crowd. It is also important to communicate your mission to your crowd, which we will take a closer look at in Chapter 5.

Armed with your mission statement, take a look at your current activity on social media.

- Does the content that you're sharing reflect how you want your business to be perceived?
- Does it clearly communicate the products or services that you offer?
- Does it convey your area of expertise?

- Does the tone of your social media mirror your approach to your customers?

If the answer to any of these questions is no, then consider the changes you can make so that your social media activity aligns with your mission. It may be that you realise you aren't promoting your products or services enough on social media, which is a trap that many fall into. Or perhaps you're using a tone of voice in your social media posts that's contrasts how you approach customers in real life. Whatever your findings, do not beat yourself up for any 'mistakes' you feel you've made. You can now move forward with a purpose and start making more strategic decisions that are in line with your mission.

If you're starting out on social media for the first time, then you have the opportunity now to lay this groundwork and allow your activity to be guided by your mission right from the start.

As you work through this exercise, remember to note your mission, your reflections on your current activity and any action points you decide upon in your strategy document, as doing so will help you ensure that your map is current and as useful as possible.

Mapping The Customer Journey

Every individual person that follows you on social media is embarking on a journey towards becoming one of your customers. There will be different starting points, and some will take detours along the way but, in basic terms, each individual will go from a point of discovering your business for the first time and will then move towards making their first purchase.

For some, this journey may involve following you on just one social media platform, engaging with your posts in one way or another and they may even buy from you without ever having left that platform.

However, for many the journey is much more complex, with multiple touch points along the way. They may follow you on more than one social media platform, read your blog posts, visit other areas of your website and even sign up to your email list. It is this complex path to purchase that can lead to some frustration over measuring return on investment, since it's often not possible to trace the customer's journey exactly or to attribute a purchase to one particular touch point.

Rather than treating each aspect of your marketing strategy, including social media, in silo, acknowledge them as points on your customer's journey. Not only does this approach prime you for success, it allows you to invest your time and energy more effectively. For example, each time you create a piece of content for social media, consider how you can reinforce that message in your email newsletter, a blog post, a video or on a different social media channel. Likewise, your social media presence can feed into other aspects of your online marketing, for example, by adding subscribers to your email list or driving more traffic to your website. You can map out how each aspect of your online marketing will interact with and be supported by your social media activity within your strategy.

Choosing Platforms Based On Purpose

The social media platforms that you use for business should, primarily, be based on where your ideal clients spend their time online and the places where they are open to engaging with businesses. In Chapter 2 we looked at understanding who your ideal clients are and where they hang out, and in Chapter 4 we'll look at the features and benefits of the most popular social media channels, but I mention it now as well because your mission should also have an influence on your choice of social media platforms, as well as how you make use of each one.

You can make a decision to use a particular social media platform because your crowd spend time there and yet still find yourself lost and unsure of where it fits into your strategy if you haven't assigned a purpose, or purposes, to it. You can attract an audience but if you don't know the path that you want to guide them along then you may well find yourself scratching your head wondering why your customer base isn't growing at the same rate as your social media followers.

I mentioned Twitter in Chapter 1 as the number one platform that people tell me they are frustrated with and often avoid because they are unsure of its purpose. LinkedIn is another platform that comes up time and time again, with many business owners telling me that they feel they 'should' be using but they are not sure why. You could well decide to go ahead and build your crowd on these platforms whilst you figure out where it fits into the customer journey and the benefits it can bring to your business, but such an approach risks you wasting your valuable time and resources. Although your understanding will grow and your strategy will evolve over time, getting clear on your purpose in using each platform, as early as possible, will reduce the likelihood of unnecessary and, potentially, costly mistakes.

The purpose that you have also needs to be shaped by the platform itself. Your understanding of what does and does not work for your business on each social media platform you use will develop over time as you put your ideas to the test. Having said that, a basic understanding of the platforms, their features, benefits and limitations will help you make sound decisions at this early stage. You can refer to Chapter 4 for a detailed guide to the most popular social media platforms but, for now, let's take Facebook as an example.

Facebook is one of the most comprehensive social media platforms for businesses, thanks to the vast array of features and tools it places at our disposal. You could say that it is all-singing and all-dancing, and the temptation can be to believe it can accommodate all of your business needs. Indeed, I know many a business owner who has built a successful business on Facebook alone so it is entirely possible. However, for other businesses it doesn't tick every box.

Take my own business, for example. One of my marketing objectives is to drive traffic to my blog, where I can nurture my readers, educate them and build trust beyond social media. If I were to rely on Facebook to drive this website traffic, without any paid advertising, it's fair to say I would have very few readers. The reason why is because Facebook's priority is to keep people on Facebook. They don't want Facebook users to leave the app or site to view content elsewhere; they want to keep you on the platform for as long as possible. For that reason, if you post a link to an external website on your Facebook Page you will, more than likely, find that your organic reach - that is the number of people who are shown that post in the Newsfeed without you paying to promote it - will be less than the reach of your other Facebook posts. So, I can do a great deal to nurture my followers on Facebook, but if I want to increase my blog readership then I cannot rely on Facebook alone. To reach a wider audience I need to consider other platforms that will allow my links to reach more of the right people, and focus my efforts on Facebook on achieving other objectives.

For each social media platform that I use, therefore, I have a clear purpose and that will shape the way that I use it. If I turn to Twitter to drive traffic to my blog, then I will be focusing much of my time on crafting engaging tweets that encourage the right people to click through and, when I come to measure my success, I will be basing this primarily on the number of clicks through to my website.

Of course, one platform may tick more than one box, but the important thing is that the purpose influences the action I take.

Making Social Media A Priority

With social media connected to your mission and a clear purpose in mind for each platform that you use, social media should, by now, feel like a priority within your business.

However, when you're in the trenches implementing your social media strategy day-in day-out, the investment of time that it demands can often become a stumbling block. The groundwork you have laid in your social media strategy means that hopefully you are not spending your time in the wrong places, but you may still get the creeping feeling that your time could be better spent elsewhere. This is a matter of both purpose and priorities.

If you've started to feel frustrated with social media or noticed that you've backed away from it then the first thing to check in with is your purpose on each platform. It could be that the purpose you had in mind is slightly off; what you thought you could achieve on a particular platform hasn't proved possible. Consider whether this is due to the limitations of the platforms, as with my example of Facebook, or the way that you're using it. Refer back to your strategy, journal your thoughts and decide on your next actions.

The other potential cause of your lacklustre social media efforts could be that it has slipped off your priority list. You're a busy business owner and you have many different plates to keep spinning all of the time, social media being just one. You might find yourself thinking how much better the results would be if you could only find the time.

The truth is, we all have the same number of hours in the day. It's not possible to find or create more hours, but you can decide how best to make use of them.

It may be that you can make more time for social media by delegating; whether that means outsourcing something else to free up time for social media or outsourcing an element of your social media. Having said that, if you're reading this book then I believe you're an entrepreneur who wants to be in the driving seat and include your energy, at least to some extent, in your social media marketing. If that's the case, then you have to make social media a priority on your to do list.

I know that that's easier said than done, believe me! As a social media manager I wouldn't blame you for assuming that my social media has always been top notch. It should be, of course, but as much as I want to walk my talk, I must confess that in the early years of my business I fell into the trap of failing to prioritise my own marketing. I knew what to do to get results on social media but I was only prioritising those results for my clients and allowing my own social media to fall by the wayside. I know how easy it is to get into this bad habit because I've had countless conversations with other entrepreneurs who have shared similar stories with me.

Naturally, my clients were and still are my number one priority but I came to realise that my own marketing must share that top spot. If I don't invest the time into working on my business, as well as in it, then I can't help the people I am here to help, which means I'm not serving my mission.

Your crowd are out there somewhere and they're waiting to hear from you. If you can reach them via social media, then why aren't you making it a priority? Why aren't you carving out the time? After all, aren't they the people you're here to serve?

Bringing It All Together

So we've reached the end of Chapter 3 and now you know the importance of having a purpose, not only for your social media as a whole but for each element of it. If you haven't written down your mission yet and taken some time to reflect on how your social media strategy aligns with that mission, then now is a good time to do so.

Once you've worked through the exercises in this chapter, as well as Chapter 2 take a look at any social media pages or profiles you already have set up. In particular, I want you to review your biographies and about sections in light of your ideal client notes and the mission statement you've drafted. Here are some questions to consider:

- Are you speaking, first and foremost, to your clients' struggles and desires?
- Are you using language that your ideal clients will understand and resonate with?
- Are you giving them a clear reason to follow you?
- Can people easily find out who's behind the business and why they should trust you?

Refer to your mission statement so that your purpose remains in focus, but don't be tempted to simply copy and paste it into your profiles. Your mission statement is a guiding light for your business, not for your customers. There may be places that you can share it with your customers on social media and on your website, but it's often more effective to turn

your mission on its head and speak directly to
wants and needs, rather than your own.

We're now going to move on to talk about your content strategy, including how to create content with purpose, what types of content you might consider utilising and why it's important to have a balanced content mix.

Chapter 4 – The Social Media Supermarket

When you're first starting out on social media, it's natural to be drawn to the platforms that you are familiar and feel comfortable with. It's certainly a great place to start because that initial familiarity and knowledge of the platform, no matter how limited or vast it may be, can help you get out of the starting blocks. As we discussed in Chapter 1, it may also mean that you already have a network of friends and family online to tap into to help get your message out there in the early days.

However, I hope that by now you are starting to understand that your long-term success on social media hinges on you having a well-thought-out strategy. It is important that you start to make strategic decisions about where you invest your time and resources on social media, moving beyond your own personal preferences. It's not just a matter of the results you can expect from your social media marketing; it's about making the best possible use of the resources you have.

No matter what stage you are at in business one thing is for sure; your time, and the time of your employees - if you are at that point - is precious. Managing your social media marketing is just one element of your job, or your employee's role if you have delegated it, so I'm sure that you can't afford to waste time. One of the biggest reasons that social media becomes a time drain for businesses is because they are focusing on the wrong platforms. The other main cause is a lack of purpose. And this isn't just a matter of how you invest your time. When you start to invest money into creating content and into advertising on social media, you want to be damn sure that you're spending in the right places. No one wants to throw money down the drain… or leave it on the table! In other words, if you're investing in the wrong places then not only is it a waste of time and resources, it could be that you're missing out on other opportunities as well.

How To Choose The Right Social Media Platforms

The obvious place to start when making this decision, and it should be a decision that you review regularly, is by reflecting on your ideal clients. In Chapter 2, I asked you to research where your ideal clients are hanging out on social media. For most businesses, your primary objective will be to reach your ideal clients, build relationships with them and, ultimately, convert them into customers, so it makes sense to focus your efforts on the platforms that they use. However, bear in mind that the purpose of your social media marketing won't always be to connect directly with your ideal clients and the immediate return on investment won't always be monetary.

Let's take Twitter as an example. Your ideal clients may hang out there, in which case it's a great platform on which to connect with them, but what if this isn't the case? If you know that your crowd aren't big tweeters then is this enough reason to leave Twitter out of your strategy? In fact, it may still have a valuable role to play so it's important to consider each platform from many different angles. You could, for example, be able to connect with journalists on Twitter, which might allow you to secure PR coverage in the publications that your ideal clients read, helping you to reach the right audience indirectly whilst also adding credibility to your business. We'll take a closer look at Twitter, and other social media platforms, in the pages that follow but, for now, I want you to be mindful of looking at the bigger picture when deciding on which platforms to utilise and dig that bit deeper into each platform's merits before you make your decision.

How Many Social Media Accounts Should You Have?

There is no magic number when it comes to how many social media accounts you can or should have, but it is vital that you are realistic about the resources you have to invest. If you know that you have limited time, especially if you know you need to invest time into learning how to use the platforms more effectively, then I recommend focusing on just one or two until you're ready to expand your efforts.

It's better to use one platform effectively than to try to juggle multiple platforms mediocrely.

You are embarking on a journey and there is no reason why you have to be everywhere right from the start. In fact, you will often find that many big brands and 'social media influencers' have a stellar presence on one platform and use other platforms to feed into this.

You can take a similar approach by making a distinction between primary and secondary platforms. Let's say that your crowd spend most of their time on Facebook and you have found this to be the best place to connect with them directly. You've also recognised that you are able to use Twitter to connect with the media, as in my example above. In this case, you may invest most of your time and resources in to Facebook, as your primary platform, whilst utilising Twitter as a secondary platform with a secondary objective. We will talk more about expanding your strategy and adding additional platforms into the mix when we discuss up-levelling in Chapter 8.

One caveat is that if you have secondary platforms, or platforms where your plan is to just have a 'presence', check in with your strategy regularly to make sure you are not paying lip service to them. You may set your Tweets up using a tool that automates their scheduling, so that you can effectively 'set and forget' Twitter, but if you check in and find that you're not getting anything at all back from it and it's not achieving the purpose you assigned it then you are still wasting valuable time and energy.

What's more, keep in mind that everything you put out on social media can be found by potential customers. They may not actively spend their time on your secondary platforms, but they could still stumble across them through online search results or by having a nosey around the links on your website. Be sure that each and every one of your social media accounts is sending out the right message and making a positive impression on whoever might come across it. I also recommend regularly searching for your business name online as this can surface long-forgotten social media accounts. You may have abandoned them but they are still out there and they are representing your brand.

The Social Media Supermarket

This book is designed to help you craft your social media strategy and I'd love for it to become your handbook; a place where you can check back in each time you review your strategy so that you continue to evolve and grow your presence on social media. For that reason, we are not going to explore the nitty-gritty specifics of each platform as the social media scene changes by the day. You can however, find stacks of support, advice and insights into different social media platforms over on my website – check out the Connect With The Author page for the link.

What we will look at, however, is the social media supermarket and what's on the shelves for you right now. We are going to consider each of the most popular platforms that are there and what your key considerations should be for each of them.

I'm especially keen to challenge the preconceptions that you might have about certain platforms, as this will help you make informed and strategic decisions to pave the way for your success.

Facebook

Facebook is without a doubt the biggest social media platform in the world right now. At the time of writing, Facebook has 1.32 billion daily active users on average.[1] Considering there were 3.8 billion internet users globally as of April 2017[2] , that is huge, and it shows little sign of slowing down any time soon.

---

[1] *https://investor.fb.com/investor-news/press-release-details/2017/Facebook-Reports-Second-Quarter-2017-Results/default.aspx*
[2] *https://thenextweb.com/contributors/2017/04/11/current-global-state-internet)*

Ignore Facebook at your peril

I know that many of you reading this will already be convinced by the value that Facebook brings to your social media strategy. As I mentioned at the beginning of the chapter, it's natural to start in the place you feel most comfortable and for many of us that place is Facebook.

However, if your marketing is Business to Business (B2B) then you may have disregarded Facebook because you don't perceive it as the best way to reach other businesses. Going back just a few years, you would probably have been right. Facebook was not, historically, the ideal place to reach other businesses and so it gained a reputation as a Business to Consumer (B2C) platforms. Now, however, that is no longer true.

Over the past few years, there has been an increasing crossover of personal and business use of Facebook.

For one thing, you can only (legally) market your business on Facebook via a Facebook Business Page but that page must be run by a legitimate personal Facebook Profile. That means that there are real people behind most Facebook Page. This has always been the case but one of the biggest game changers has been the rise of Facebook Groups.

As of June 2017, there were more than 1 billion people[3] using Groups every month and, at their first Communities Summit in 2017, Facebook explained how committed they are to prioritising communities on Facebook.

Up until recently, it has only been possible to interact in Facebook Groups via a personal Profile. Although Facebook Pages are now being brought into the fold, people have become accustomed to using Groups

---

[3] *https://newsroom.fb.com/news/2017/06/two-billion-people-coming-together-on-facebook*

personally and I expect that this will continue, although we may see more interaction from Pages in Groups as well.

In years gone by, the drawback of Facebook was the difficulty in connecting with other businesses and, in particular, with decision makers within those businesses. After all, even if your marketing is B2B you are, nevertheless, trying to reach real life people, and, in particular, people with the power to decide whether to invest in your product or service. Business people are increasingly using Facebook as individuals, as well as brands, and the lines are blurring between business and personal use. This means that there is more opportunity than ever before on Facebook for you to connect with your ideal clients, whether they are businesses or consumers.

In fact, 90% of new business I have generated over the past 12 months has been through Facebook.

There are other touch points involved, with people often following and engaging with me across multiple platforms and different marketing channels, but Facebook has been the primary driver. What's more, only around half of the leads I've generated have come directly through my Facebook Page. The other 50% have been through Facebook Groups, and the journey there is even more complex. Often the initial contact I have with a potential customer is through a Facebook Group. This is absolutely non-sales related. I invest a lot of my time into conversations with people in Facebook Groups, answering questions and offering advice absolutely free of charge, pitch-free and with no catch whatsoever. You might think I'm mad for giving so much advice and support away for free but it's the best marketing investment I could possibly make in my business. The people that I help often go on to find my Facebook Page. Again, I never ever pitch this; I'm not asking people to come over to my Facebook Page because we've had a conversation in a Group and I'm not saying 'send me a PM if you want to find out more'. Either, they will do a little digging themselves and find the link via my personal Profile (again, blurred lines!) or someone else will point them in my direction because my dedication to these business-related Groups has positioned me as their go-to resource.

It's about having patience and being in it for the long-haul. If you post a sales pitch and run off to the next group to do the same, what makes you think the other Group members, who more than likely have no idea who you are, will buy from you? They won't. It takes time for people to get to know who you are, and what your business has to offer, and even more time for them to trust you enough to buy. What's more, if someone never goes on to work with me but I've been able to help them, in a small way, in a Facebook

Group then I'm still happy because that's still aligned with my mission.

With Facebook placing increasing emphasis on the role of Groups on the platform, and the success stories I've witnessed and been involved with time and time again, I'd suggest that your Facebook strategy needs to utilise both your Page and Groups if you want to get the best results possible. Be reassured, it gets easier over time and as you and your business become more well-known you will have less leg work to do as people will increasingly come to you, but at first you must be prepared to go to them.

The final thought I'd like to share about Facebook, and particularly about Facebook Groups, is that it can be not only an element of your marketing strategy but a huge source of support for you and your business. The network of entrepreneurs that I've built on Facebook has become an invaluable part of the day-to-day running of my business. Not only have I met clients, but I have also met people who help and support my business, not least entrepreneurs who have become my friends and mastermind buddies.

Instagram

In 2012, Facebook bought Instagram and since then it has grown rapidly to over 700 million users[4], with more than 250 million people[5] using Instagram Stories every day. It's safe to say that it has become the most popular visual social media platform in the world right now.

Instagram users are interested in everything from fashion to beauty, travel to food, and a whole lot more in between. What's more, it has proved itself to be a platform of influence with the rise of Instagram

---

[4] *http://blog.instagram.com/post/160011713372/170426-700million*

[5] *https://instagram-press.com/blog/2017/08/02/celebrating-one-year-of-instagram-stories*

stars who are building worldwide brands of their own, in some cases single-handedly, on the platform.

The potential seems clear when you look at the stats and the influence that prominent users have acquired through the platform, but using it effectively can be a little trickier for businesses - particularly businesses that aren't global brands with huge budgets for photography or masses of user-generated content at their disposal.

Again, if your business sells direct to consumers, particularly if you have a product that lends itself to being photographed, then you might find it somewhat easier to build a presence on Instagram, or at least it may be easier to get started.

However, if you have a product that isn't especially photogenic or you sell a service, whether to businesses or consumers, that can't easily be captured in a photograph, Instagram may seem like a non-starter for you.

In fact, whichever camp you fall into, the key to success on Instagram is creativity. Even if you have a product to photograph, your followers may get bored if all you are sharing is product shot after product shot.

What you need to do is think beyond the superficial and really dig deep into understanding the hopes, dreams and struggles of your ideal clients. The good news, of course, is that you've already laid the groundwork for this by following the exercises in Chapter 2.

One of my favourite examples of a brand that has thought outside of the box and created a beautiful and emotive Instagram feed is Buffer[6]. Buffer is a

---

[6] *https://www.instagram.com/buffer*

social media management tool; not something that lends itself to be photographed or conveyed a visual way at all really. They could have gone down the route of sharing tips or news about social media, but that's not really what their brand is about and it's not why their customers choose to use Buffer. People use Buffer because it will save them time when scheduling their social media posts, it will allow them to be more organised, more consistent and more productive. Digging even deeper into that, it frees up their time to do other things, things that they'd rather be spending their time doing. Having adventures. Their feed is nothing like you would expect; it is full of beautiful scenery, landmarks and even the occasional adorably cute animal, and it absolutely works. Social media scheduling is one of the least emotive topics you could be creating content around, and yet Buffer has made it incredibly emotive by opening up a world of adventures that its followers can explore.

Now, you may not have the budget and / or the influence that Buffer has to source mind-blowing photography, but you can invest the time in understanding who your ideal clients are and what content resonates with them in a meaningful way.

As with each platform you introduce into your social media strategy, you should also consider your purpose. Perhaps an element of your purpose will be to build that all important trust with your crowd. How can you do this on Instagram?

- Consider sharing photos and videos from behind the scenes.
- Show people what goes into making your product or delivering your service.
- Give your followers the opportunity to get to know the people behind the business.
- Engage with them person-to-person rather than business-to-customer.

My overriding advice about Instagram would be that, whatever your approach to creating content, you should have a principal theme that encompasses and guides everything that you post. Spontaneous posts are great, but if they don't add to your overall theme then they could cause confusion amongst your followers.

A good check-in point is to look at the first 12 images on your Instagram feed and ask yourself; if someone came across this and knew nothing else about me or my business would they be able to tell what my account is about? You might have shared a beautiful photo that you took when you were on holiday, for example, but does it make your theme clearer or fuzzier? It's not to say that you can't use that photo anywhere on social media, but when it comes to Instagram you will find times when it's necessary to be highly selective in your content choices.

So, whilst Instagram, much like every other platform we're going to consider, will no doubt evolve over the coming years, a deep understanding of your crowd and the willingness to think creatively to produce content that will resonate with them will always stand you in good stead.

Twitter

Unlike the other social media platforms we have covered so far, Twitter does not openly reveal exact Daily Active User figures for the platform, although it has recently stated that both Daily Users and Monthly Active Usage is on the increase[7]. You don't necessarily need to get hung up on usage figures. What is more important is whether Twitter could be effective in helping you to reach your ideal clients, or other users who may indirectly help you to reach your

---

[7] *http://files.shareholder.com/downloads/AMDA-2F526X/4861728019x0x951003/11DEB964-E7A5-43F8-96E2-D074A947255B/TWTR_Q2_17_Earnings_Press_Release.pdf*

crowd. It's good to be aware of reports that Twitter is, at best, plateauing, and at worst in decline, and that it is certainly not growing at the same rate as platforms such as Instagram, but that does not necessarily mean it's wise to ignore Twitter.

I expect you are less concerned about the usage figures and more concerned about the value that Twitter can bring to your business. Whilst I have spoken to many entrepreneurs who still love the platform, and others who can't abide it, I have had conversations with many more people who tell me they have fallen out of love with Twitter or that they outright avoid it. The reasons for this are many and varied, here are just a few of the comments people have shared with me of late;

- I can't work out how to reach my crowd
- It's too time-consuming to create and schedule 'enough' Tweets

- Twitter moves too quickly
- It feels impersonal
- I feel that the only way to make it work is to send people somewhere with a direct link
- I hate the character limit
- It seems difficult to build relationships on Twitter; I feel like I'm being sold to all the time
- I never get any enquiries on Twitter
- I find the whole thing where you get unfollowed if you don't follow back is annoying

Lots of these reservations about Twitter are practical, such as struggling to find the time or finding it difficult to convey a message in a limited space. These are actually the easiest stumbling blocks to overcome and you'll find stacks of advice and ideas to help you in this respect over on my blog.

What I want to discuss here is those misgivings about Twitter that are a little less tangible; the concerns that hold you back from using the platform at all.

I have lost count of how many people feel that Twitter is impersonal, so it's clearly a major stumbling block. I completely understand why so many people have this impression of Twitter but it doesn't have to be that way. You can use Twitter to connect with genuine people, people who aren't purely interested in getting you to follow or pitching something to you. You can have meaningful conversations and build relationships with people who will bring benefit to your business, whether they are potential customers, journalists, other entrepreneurs whom you can draw on for support, potential suppliers... the list goes on.

If you decide that Twitter will be one of your primary or secondary social media platforms, then, as with every platform you are utilising, your starting point should be deciding upon its purpose. Twitter, perhaps more so than any of the other platforms we are going to consider here, can have multiple and varied purposes that feed into your social media strategy. Your goals may include;

- Nurturing ideal clients who follow you elsewhere on social media by adding Twitter as an additional touch point to their customer journey.
- Driving traffic to your website. Given the fact that Facebook limits the organic reach of external links and Instagram provides limited opportunities for you to share clickable links, Twitter could be an excellent supplement that will help you to drive more traffic to your website.
- Connect with the media, journalists and bloggers to secure PR opportunities for your business.

- Engage with other thought-leaders in your industry and raise your own profile as an expert in your field.
- Build relationships with potential suppliers, joint venture partners and other entrepreneurs who you may be able to work with in the future.

This list is not exhaustive by any means and it is varied, but if I were to choose one word to sum up the purpose of Twitter to your business it would be - networking.

Twitter allows you to connect with such a wide array of people, more directly and quicker than often is the case on other social media platforms, and who amongst us would not benefit from increasing our professional network? The return you see from Twitter may not always be immediate and it may not be as tangible as increased revenue, but when you invest in your professional network you will be amazed at the opportunities that present themselves in the future, even when you're not expecting it.

LinkedIn

As with Twitter, LinkedIn does not publish Daily Active User or Monthly Active User figures but what we do know is that they hit the 500 million total user mark in early 2017[8]. It may seem like a drop in the ocean compared to the likes of Facebook and Instagram, but LinkedIn is, nevertheless, worthy of your consideration. After all, LinkedIn continues to be the world's leading professional social network.

And yet, the mere mention of LinkedIn often invokes much the same feedback as Twitter. In fact, the sentiment is often stronger; some people love it, many people seem to hate it and others avoid it

---

[8] *https://blog.linkedin.com/2017/april/24/the-power-of-linkedins-500-million-community*

altogether. Unlike Twitter, however, many of the entrepreneurs I speak to recognise the value of LinkedIn and have an underlying feeling that they 'should' be there... but they simply don't want to be.

I could tell you to put your personal feelings about LinkedIn aside and get on with it if it can help you to grow your business, but I know that is not entirely realistic for many people. Yes, you might take it on board and give LinkedIn a shot, but if you strongly dislike the platform I would bet money that you will inevitably lose interest and go back to ignoring it.

The truth of the matter is, we aren't robots who can programme our strategy into our brains and follow it to the letter, come what may. If you're not enjoying using a particular social media platform, then, at best, you won't get the most out of it and, at worst, it will fall by the wayside. I also know that you may never come to adore LinkedIn, but you can learn to like it and make better use of it.

So why is it that some people have such a strong dislike of LinkedIn?

Again, there are many and varied reasons but one that comes up time and time again is that people don't like the 'rules' of LinkedIn and feel like they can't be true to themselves on this platform.

There is a perception that you must uphold a 'professional' image on LinkedIn; after all, it is a professional network, right? There are certainly vocal LinkedIn users who beseech people not to bring Facebook practices over to LinkedIn and decry anyone who dares to add personality or personal opinion to their posts. But what is the point in using LinkedIn if you have to create a false persona to fit in?

The truth is, you don't need to.

For starters, as an entrepreneur your LinkedIn Profile is not an online CV. Your purpose is not to find a job, and utilising your Profile as a CV is not going to resonate with your ideal clients. Instead, think of your Profile as an extension of the about page on your website. You can use it to communicate your mission, to relate to your ideal clients, to showcase your work and to add credibility by sharing the *relevant* experience and qualifications you have gained. You do not need to list every job you've ever had or what school you went to, unless they are absolutely relevant to the people you're trying to connect with.

When it comes to sharing content on LinkedIn, there is no reason why it cannot be an extension of the social media strategy you implement on other social media platforms. In fact, it absolutely should be. If one of your Facebook followers, for example, stumbled across your LinkedIn profile they should feel like they are connecting with exactly the same person and brand as they have connected with on Facebook. If you're presenting a version of yourself that is alien to them, then they're going to be left feeling confused and perhaps even a little mistrustful of who you really are.

What's more, it's simply a pointless exercise. If you filter your brand, your personality and the content you share to fit in with what you perceive as the 'professional' standards of LinkedIn then you will inevitably attract the wrong people. They will not be your ideal clients.

Realising that you don't need to create a professional persona for LinkedIn is the first step in beginning to enjoy using the platform. If you don't want to encounter those people who preach about the so-called rules then you can remove them from your network. Be reassured that there are plenty of people on LinkedIn, soulful entrepreneurs just like me and you, who are there to spread their message in a genuine way and connect with like-minded people.

Of course, there are some strategies that work on other social media platforms that won't work as well on LinkedIn, so I'm not suggesting that you replicate your Facebook strategy exactly. For example, memes are not a big hit on LinkedIn but opinion pieces, or as I refer to them 'mini blogs', can work exceptionally well. Spend some time connecting with people on LinkedIn, observe how they use the platform and then take your existing social media content as a starting point and begin to test which posts work well for you on LinkedIn.

If you make the decision that LinkedIn is not going to be a platform that you invest in, it's still important that you don't let your Profile, if you have one, gather dust. LinkedIn Profiles often rank very highly in online search results, so if someone pops your name into a search engine then there's good chance that your LinkedIn Profile will pop up. Even if you're not active on LinkedIn, your Profile may leave a lasting impression on that person. At the very least, if you have a LinkedIn Profile, ensure that it is regularly updated and continues to reflect your brand in the best possible way.

Bringing It All Together

Throughout the course of this chapter we have covered four of the major platforms in the social media supermarket. It would be impossible to cover the entire multitude of social media platforms here and the social media scene will most certainly continue to change and evolve. However, what I have done here is given you an insight into four of the most popular social media platforms in the world and how to evaluate the value that they can bring to your business. Taking this on board, you can ask the same questions of other social media platforms and expand your strategy to encompass others.

If you need additional support getting to grips with specific platforms then you can find additional resources over on my website.

Chapter 5 – Creating Content

Content is the linchpin that holds your entire social media strategy together and yet it's often the most difficult element to manage. When you are at your most creative and inspired, creating content can be a breeze but there will also be times when inspiration alludes you and keeping up with the task of creating fresh, interesting and engaging content feels like wading through treacle.

In the chapters that follow, we're going to tackle the whole content creation challenge and you will walk away armed with strategies that will keep you inspired, productive and consistent from now on.

Creating Content With Purpose

We've talked a lot about purpose already and it's going to come up time and time again in this chapter.

I also want you to keep that word in the back of your mind each and every time you create a piece of content.

Every time you're creating a piece of content, ask yourself what purpose it is serving;

- Is it helping your crowd in some way? This could be anything from teaching them something, offering reassurance and even making them laugh.
- Is it going to attract new people into your crowd?
- Is it demonstrating your expertise?
- Is it showing, rather than telling, what you have to offer to your ideal clients?

There are many more purposes that your content might have and some posts will tick more than one box. The important thing is that each post serves a real purpose and fits within your overall social media strategy. In other words, you are not posting something just to fill a gap or a silence but, rather, each post is bringing you closer to achieving your goals.

With that in mind, when you are in content creation mode, continue your questioning with;

So what?

- Why is what you're sharing worthy of being read or watched?
- Why should your crowd care about it?
- What is it about that piece of content which will capture people's attention?
- What message does it convey?
- And how does that support your overall strategy?

Here are some examples of how individual posts and different types of content might fit into your social media strategy;

- Sharing a tip or piece of advice demonstrates your knowledge and gives your crowd a taste of how you can help them.
- Face-to-camera video blogs help people to get to know you and your way of working, which can help them make a decision as to whether working with you is right for them.
- 'Mini-blogs' are longer social media posts that can help your ideal clients to identify their pain points and the outcomes that you can help them to achieve. It can give them the sense that there is a solution that will meet their needs.
- Testimonials, reviews and case studies provide social proof and also help to set

expectations; if people don't know what to expect from working with you, both in terms of the experience and the outcomes, then they may well be reluctant to buy.

- Behind the scenes posts show the people behind your brand and help to build the know, like and trust factor.

Keeping this thought process in mind, let's take a look at some of the different types of content you can use within your social media strategy.

The Rise and Rise of Video

Had I been writing this book just 18 months earlier, video may have sat way down this list and yet here it is, sitting pretty right at the top!

Of course, video has been around on social media for a long time but it only really started to dominate the scene in 2016. I won't bore you with the long and winding history of social video here but a major game-changer came when Facebook began rolling out live streaming to the general public in January 2016 (it had been available to verified public figures since August 2015).

Live streaming invites all of us to become broadcasters; not only communicating our message in video form but allowing us to engage in real-time conversation with our followers. That's an amazing opportunity.

In fact, in an interview with Buzzfeed[9] when Facebook Live became available to most users in April 2016, Mark Zuckerberg himself said: 'I wouldn't be surprised if you fast-forward five years and most of the content that people see on Facebook and are sharing on a day-to-day basis is video.'

---

[9] *https://www.buzzfeed.com/mathonan/why-facebook-and-mark-zuckerberg-went-all-in-on-live-video*

So it seems pretty obvious that video should be the star of your content strategy, right?

Actually, it's not as clear cut as marketers thought it might be when Facebook changed the game. Video and live streaming hasn't eclipsed all other types of content and I honestly don't think it ever will, at least not entirely. I'm going to talk in a lot more detail, towards the end of this Chapter, about balancing your content mix and the importance of utilising different types of content, but the point I want to make here is this:

Not everyone loves watching videos

I happen to have a bit of wandering mind and a short attention span when it comes to watching media and it takes a lot to keep me engaged (don't ever try to watch a film with me, I'm a talker!). There are exceptions but most of the time I would prefer to read instead of watch.

And then you have people who love watching video but there are times when they aren't able to or don't want to watch. If they're just having a quick flick through the Newsfeed whilst sat in the doctor's waiting room then they're more likely to scroll past videos, whereas a short and snappy text post or an eye-catching image may well catch their attention.

Becoming Comfortable With Being On Camera

If you've ever struggled to write your thoughts out in the form of blog posts or even short social media posts, video offers an outlet to express your message more freely and in a way that may feel more natural to you.

If you're happy and confident with being on camera then fantastic – embrace it and crack on! But if video is outside of your comfort zone, as I know it is for many people, then that doesn't mean it's off limits to you.

The first time I recorded a video I lost count of how many takes it took me. The first time I went live on my Facebook Page I was shaking with nerves and talking at a hundred miles an hour! In fact, it's amazing how quickly that discomfort comes back if I leave it too long between videos.

The same issues come up time and time again when I'm coaching clients one to one. So often when I ask them how they feel about video they launch into telling me they know they need to start using video, they're planning on doing it but a lack of confidence, whether that's confidence in front of the camera or with the technical aspect of recording and editing, is holding them back.

If this is the position you're in right now, then the best thing you can do is get started. As long as it's sat on your to-do list being ignored or put off it will not get any easier.

The age-old adage 'practice makes perfect' rings true here.

So grab your phone or webcam and a reasonably bright desk lamp, because you don't need fancy equipment to get started, and hit record.

Don't jump straight into a live broadcast and don't put any pressure on yourself to produce a video that you feel is good enough to share publicly. This is purely about practicing and getting comfortable with talking to camera because, of course, it's going to feel a little odd and unnatural at first. You don't even need to worry about what you're saying at this point; talk about your business or run through what you've done with your day, just get used to talking to the camera like you would talk to a customer if they were stood in front of you.

The goal is for you to feel comfortable talking to your crowd via video in a way that is natural and genuine.

When you're ready to start doing this you will be amazed at the connections you can make with your followers. Video allows your crowd to get to know you, like you and trust you like nothing else. They are able to get a real feel for the person or people behind the brand, your way of working, and the help or support you have to offer to your customers.

Be Creative With Your Videos

Up until this point I have been talking, primarily, about what you might call video blogs. In other words, you or someone within your business talking directly to camera about a topic that would naturally lend itself to a blog – advice, top tips, lessons or news from your business, for example.

But, of course, that's not the only way to use video, although for many businesses it is one of the most effective.

As you become more comfortable with creating videos, particularly with planning and editing them, challenge yourself to think creatively about how you might communicate your message via video. Here are a few ideas to get you started but, really, the possibilities are endless:

- Transform blog posts into animated videos (Lumen5[10] is a great tool to use for this)
- Demonstrate your product
- Ask customers for video testimonials
- Interview an expert in a complementary field
- Use a free online GIF maker to create short, funny videos

[10] *https://lumen5.com*

Making The Most Of Memes

Memes are images or videos overlaid with a caption or quote. Over the past few years, they have become a popular form of social media content, used by publishers, businesses and the general public. They are often designed to be humorous and entertaining, although their use has evolved to include motivational and inspirational quotes, which work particularly well on business pages. This type of content can be highly sharable, thanks to its simplicity and the entertaining or inspiring nature of the meme.

However, as with any type of content you are publishing on social media, it's important to be mindful of the purpose that your memes serve. The key is to avoid posting content for the sake of it.

When creating memes and constructing the posts that accompany your meme, consider what purpose that post is serving.

No doubt you will have seen a funny meme go viral on social media, whether you were aware of it or not - a dead giveaway is that feeling that you can't seem to escape the post, it keeps popping up time and time again in your feed, shared and liked by different people. As a business, however, virality may seem like a desirable achievement but what purpose does that actually serve to your business? Are you chasing big numbers in the hope that it will get your business attention and added credibility? Although it can seem this way at times, social media marketing is not a numbers game. Getting thousands or even millions of eyes on a post only benefits your business if they are the right eyes. If that meme you posted has no bearing on your overall message and no specific appeal to your ideal clients then it might give a one-time hit of engagement and even new followers, but it's not likely to bring a long-term benefit to your business.

The golden rule of quality and quantity should always win out when you're building a soulful and sustainable social media presence.

Instead of chasing the numbers, think about how your memes can bring tangible value to your crowd. What's more, with so many other Facebook Pages, not to mention personal accounts, sharing memes if you don't have a purpose and a unique message to share then your memes will be easily overlooked.

So instead of just posting a meme on its own, think about whether:

- That inspirational quote could be used as a starting point for you to share a lesson with your crowd.
- Add more to the conversation than just the quote in order to demonstrate your knowledge, expertise and the ways in which you can help your followers.

- Consider creating a humorous image that helps them to identify a problem or struggle they're experiencing in a relatable way.

Let The Words Do The Talking

So far we have focused on multimedia and I know that many people are reluctant to post anything that isn't accompanied by some form of media. Not all that long ago, that was the advice you would hear from most social media experts but the landscape has evolved and I would be very cautious about following any 'golden rules' like that now.

There really is no one-size-fits-all when it comes to social media.

I will go on to explain how different post types may improve or lessen your chances of being seen but, for now, I want to tell you that sometimes it's OK, in fact it can be more effective, to simply let your words do the talking.

If you're scrambling to find a photo or video to add to a post you've already written and it's really just for the sake of making sure there is some multimedia included, then it may actually detract from your message rather than add value.

Since there are no golden rules to follow, allow yourself to be led by the content. If a post can stand alone with only words then allow it to do so. Equally, be mindful of the fact that adding media to a post can sometimes make it less engaging if it has the feel of an advert. For example, questions and conversation starters often work best as text-only posts because adding an image can make it feel more business-like and therefore less genuine to some people.

Crafting A Balanced Content Mix

I hope that your creative juices are flowing by now, you're ready and raring to go and you're excited about the vast array of possibilities there are for your social media content.

What you will no doubt find is that you lean more towards some types of content than others. This will, in part, come down to what you feel comfortable creating and sharing but it is important that you allow your decisions to be guided by the wants and needs of your crowd, rather than entirely by your own personal preferences. After all, this is all about them really. If you only create video, because that's where you feel most comfortable, then you risk losing people's interest if they aren't engaged video watchers.

As you learn more about your ideal clients and try and test different content types on your social media accounts, you will gain a better understanding of what works for your crowd and your business. In Chapter 8, we will take a closer look at how you can use analytics to test and evolve your strategy, but when you're first starting out my advice is to ensure that no one content type is excluded. In fact, even as you test and tweak your strategy, there will still be a place for most types of content within your mix, although you may utilise some more than others. There are two key reasons for this.

The first is that different people consume information in different ways. Even though we have talked about your ideal clients as being a collective group it is, in fact, a group made up of unique individuals who have certain things in common. They will share similar struggles, pain points and desires, but I'm yet to find a group where they all share the same preferences for consuming content. More than likely, you will have people within your ideal client group who love watching videos, others who prefer audio that they can listen to on the move and others who prefer to read. And even within those sub-groups there will be preferences based on things like the length of video they engage with or the amount of text they will comfortably read, particularly on social media where often times people are in a rush.

The second reason why it is important to have a good mix of content is because most social media platforms have an algorithm in place and that algorithm will continue to change and evolve over time.

An algorithm is, according to the Oxford Dictionary, 'a process or set of rules to be followed in calculations or other problem-solving operations, especially by a computer'.

I will explain more about algorithms in Chapter 8 but, for now, all you need to know is that an algorithm decides what content to show to a user at any given time.

Content type is particularly important to the Facebook algorithm because of the wide variety of content types that Facebook supports. Facebook know that some types of content are preferred, in general over others. Over the past couple of years, video in particular has been given a great deal of preference on Facebook. That's led many people to dish out advice that the majority of your content should be video – before that, you might have been told that your posts should always include an image. But it's actually more individual than that because the algorithm also takes into account personal preferences. So, for example, if I tend to ignore videos in my Newsfeed but often click on the read more button on text-only posts and spend more time reading posts than I do looking at any other type of post, then I'm more likely to see more of those long text posts in the future. That's a simplified explanation as there are lots of other factors at play, but the key point to take away is that every individual user's Newsfeed is different and, therefore, what works and what doesn't work for every Page is different.

Again, there is no one-size-fits-all solution.

Don't rule out any one type of content to start with, if at all. I've heard people say you should never publish a text-only post on Facebook. In fact, text-only posts are often one of the most engaged with post types and achieve the best organic reach on my Facebook Page and on a number of my client's Pages. If we rule out text-only posts, without testing them, we could be missing out on valuable reach and engagement!

This might leave you feeling in a bit of a pickle if you're not sure where to start or how to decide which post types to use and when. My advice is to be led by the content, always. If your post stands alone without any image or video then publish it as it is. If it could be enhanced by an image, then add an image. If you could explain the point better in a video then post a video. In the next chapter we're also going to talk about how you can re-use and repurpose your content so that you can share the same message consistently in different formats and reach more of your ideal clients as a result.

A Place For Promotion

Thinking back to the question of purpose and where the content you create fits into your overall social media strategy, promotion is perhaps the most difficult content type to balance. Either you have too much and your crowd disengage or you have too little promotion and your followers don't convert into paying customers.

This applies to more than just the promotion of your products or services. For most businesses, driving traffic to your website is an important function of social media; from there you can encourage people to subscribe to your mailing list, educate them about your products or services and engage them with other content such as blog posts. Balance is key here also because if every post is aiming to drive traffic away from the social media platform and onto your website you will struggle to build an engaged audience on social media, but if you don't promote your website at all then your social media may be running on its own and not connecting the dots of your overall marketing strategy.

Although it will vary depending on your marketing schedule and what you are promoting at any one time, you may find it helpful to create a loose plan that will structure and balance your posts. For example, you can decide how often and when you will share links to your blog posts or when and how often you will invite people to subscribe to your newsletter.

You will find a content plan template and example in the bonus resources.

Bringing It All Together

So, in this chapter we have talked about a number of different types of content that you can produce for social media and how to maintain a balanced mix of content in order to appeal to as many of your ideal clients as possible. In the following chapter we're going to look at creating a content library and how to get the most value possible out of each and every piece of content you create. Managing your content affectively will help you make the most of the time and resources you invest into social media and it will help you to reinforce your key messages with your crowd.

Chapter 6 – Staying Sane On Social Media

By now, I hope that you are bursting with inspiration and ideas for content to share on social media! The more content that you create, however, the more important it becomes for you to fine-tune your strategy and sure up the systems and processes you have in place to help you manage your social media marketing effectively.

Creating a Content Library

The sooner you start capturing and storing your content in your own library the better!

Each and every piece of content that you create, from memes to videos, Tweets to blog posts, becomes a business asset and you should look after it like you would any other asset within your business. The bottom line is, you have invested time, energy and resources in to creating that content so don't simply hit post and move straight onto the next idea, because there is lots more value to be had in that piece of content!

We are going to go on to look at how you can make use of your content library and extract more value from your posts. But how do you create a content library in the first place?

Trello, Microsoft Excel, Word, Dropbox, Google Drive – a combination of those tools – or even your social media scheduling tool, can all be used to store your content. Just like your strategy, the important thing is to create a system that works for you because if it's not easy to manage and takes too much time then it will end up falling by the wayside.

You will also find that your process for managing content will evolve over time.

In my own business, I have experimented with lots of different systems over the years and eventually settled on Trello as my main content library – check out the Bonus Resources for a demo of how I use Trello to store and manage my content. I use Trello to store my memes (along with the text they've been shared with in the past), my top tips (also including text, images, videos and links that I've used to accompany each tip) and a library of my blog posts and videos. I also use an Excel spreadsheet to store my evergreen Tweets, which are Tweets without an obvious expiration date, as it allows for easy copy and pasting into my scheduling tool. Chunky content, including blog posts, videos and graphics, are also backed up on Dropbox. I have to say that ContentCal, the social media scheduling tool I currently use, does a fantastic job of storing my past content and allowing me to re-use posts, as do many other tools on the market. However, I find that having my own system and back-ups gives me peace of mind; should I ever switch to a different scheduling tool for any reason then I won't have to start over with my content library.

Making the Most of Your Content

The main reason I recommend creating a content library for your business is because it allows you to extract more value from every piece of content that you create.

You have poured time, energy and resources into creating your content so it is wasteful to use it once and create something new. Having said that, the value of having a content library and using it to re-use and repurpose your content reaches far beyond this.

Don't reinvent the wheel – reinforce the message

Most people need to read or hear a message more than once in order to really take it in.

For example, if you share a tip with your crowd just once then some might take it on board and action that tip straightaway, but others will forget all about it, even if it captured their attention initially.

Instead of sharing a different tip every day, what if you built upon that first message and created an experience that was more memorable and engaging?

Let's say that a day or two after you shared your tip as an image post, you then shared a video that talked me through what to do and the benefits of doing it. The idea is now planted more firmly in my mind. Then a few days later you share an example of how your tip can be used in the real world - perhaps with a case study or some feedback from someone who has tried it out themselves. Now I really can't wait to try it for myself and I'll remember that I heard it from you!

That simple tip has quickly got me to know, like and trust you, AND I may even spread the word. The bonus is that you've created stacks of valuable content from just one seed!

This is just one example, but the principle can be applied to every type of content that you create and share and doesn't necessarily have to happen over a short time span. Another strategy is to look back at your older content and consider how you can re-use and re-purpose it. Newer followers will not have seen it before and older followers will probably have forgotten about it if a few months or weeks have passed. You are not only reinforcing your message but introducing it to new people for the first time.

This is where social media analytics come into their own, and making use of them is much easier than you might think.

Let's take Facebook as an example. As well as Facebook Insights (the main analytics dashboard on your Facebook Page) you'll also find Facebook

Publishing Tools on your Page. Publishing Tools is basically a chronological library of everything you have ever posted on your Facebook Page! What makes it really useful is that it shows you, at a glance, the reach and engagement of each post. This makes it really easy to look over your past posts and pick out those that stand out as your best performers. If you feel enough time has passed, you may re-use the post in its original form but there is usually room for improvement. Before you re-post, review the original and consider tweaking the wording or updating the photo or video so that the post gets even better results this time around.

Next, think about whether you could explore that same topic in any other format. For example, could you re-purpose a written social media post into a video? Or could you compile five top tips that you originally shared on social media into a blog post? This way, you're reinforcing the message and getting more value from your content whilst still keeping your social media posts fresh and interesting.

You can also reverse engineer the process from blog posts. Let's say you've written a blog post with a list of five top tips... you can then create content around each individual tip to share on social media. You're optimising your time and you're creating more meaningful connections with your followers. Win, win!

A Word of Caution About Crossposting

Whilst I am a big advocate of re-using and repurposing content to get the most value possible out of everything you create, you should be mindful about where and when you are re-sharing content.

I often see, for example, the same post being shared on a Facebook Page, a personal profile and multiple Groups all at the same time. No matter how great the content is, seeing the same post in so many different places very close together can lead people to put their guard up. It doesn't feel genuine or organic and those two ingredients are key to getting people to engage with you on social media.

The same applies to posting across different platforms. Bear in mind that people may follow you on more than one platform and seeing the same post in these different places can turn some people off, although it may not happen immediately. Even though some platforms, such as Instagram, allow you to share your post elsewhere with just one tap, and it's easy to do the same via most social media scheduling tools, I advise you to use this option with caution. Not only can it begin to feel boring and unengaging, but it is not necessarily the best way to make the most of every platform that you're utilising.

People have different expectations on different platforms. For example, on Instagram your posts are going to be image-led and the captions are likely to include multiple hashtags. If you share that same post to LinkedIn, for example, you might find that it doesn't convey quite the same message and isn't in line with what people are looking for and engaging with on LinkedIn. Likewise, I often see Tweets that have been automatically posted from a Facebook - there is nothing more frustrating than having to click on a link to Facebook to finish reading a Tweet because it doesn't fit into Twitter's character limit.

Ultimately, when you rely too heavily on crossposting it can begin to feel like there is no real person behind the page or profile. If your followers don't feel like there is a genuine voice behind your posts then they will become wary of engaging and eventually they may switch off altogether. If you want to see results from social media then you need to have a strategy for each platform you're using and tailor your content accordingly. It's not enough to just have a 'presence' on a platform, you need to be invested in it. If you don't feel that you have the time or resources for that right now then my advice is to focus on less platforms and expand your strategy to include others when you are able to use them effectively and consistently.

What to Do When You Lose Your Way

Keeping track of your content goes a long way towards maintaining your social media sanity, but even with all that content there may be times when you find yourself struggling to stay consistent and make progress.

I've hit those roadblocks myself over the years and I've also helped many of my clients to overcome them. In fact, nine times out of ten when people first start working with me it's because they are stuck, in one way or another, with creating content for social media. The strategies that I am going to share with you in the remainder of this chapter will help to keep you on track and get you unstuck if ever you find yourself in that place.

Making Social Media Manageable

Social media marketing is a marathon not a race.

It's not a one-off marketing campaign that you can pour your energy and resources into for a fixed period of time and then regroup afterwards. It is an ongoing process that requires you and / or your team to show up consistently day-in, day-out. If you take your foot off the gas, even just for a week or two, you will no doubt see the effect it has on your results.

Fortunately, you have already taken the most important step in safeguarding your social media sanity by reading this book and using it to create a strategy for your business. Having a plan in place makes it so much easier to stay on track because you have made all of the big decisions in advance and allowed time to review them regularly. On a day-to-day basis that means that you can concentrate on creating fantastic content and nurturing your relationships with your crowd.

One element of social media strategy that we haven't touched on yet, however, is how you will implement it on a daily basis. If you're reading this then I'm assuming that you have some involvement with managing your social media, whether that means you're handling everything yourself or you have outside support helping you with it.

For most people, the biggest drain is constantly coming up with new ideas for content, for all aspects of their marketing not just social media. Whilst we have talked through the many different ways that you can re-use and re-purpose the content that you have already created, you will still need to think of new ideas because your business and your crowd will always be evolving and with it your message.

There is nothing like the frustration of staring at a blank screen and willing inspiration to strike. Or the panic of realising you haven't posted anything and you need to think of something to break the silence as soon as possible. These are the times when you might end up posting the first thing that comes to mind just to get something out there or, perhaps, you end up avoiding social media for a while. Either way, what you're doing is not helping to move your business forward.

First things first, prevention is always better than cure!

Although there may still be times when you hit a creative block, there are things you can do to reduce the risk of that happening and make your life a whole lot easier in the process.

Your content library should become your first port of call whenever you're struggling for ideas. Spend some time looking back at your older content; what haven't you talked about in a while? When have you missed an opportunity to re-purpose a piece of content? What's worked really well in the past that you could resurrect now?

The next place to turn is your ideal client journal, which we talked about back in Chapter 2. Reflect on what your ideal clients are struggling with and what they need from you right now. In particular, have a think back to the questions you've been asked over the past few weeks and the conversations that you've had; there is no better way to find out what your crowd need to hear from you than to listen to what they're asking.

Really, this is all about creating the right habits to keep you on track and make your social media marketing more of a fluid process. Get into the habit of noting down questions, feedback and conversations in your ideal client journal and get into the habit of logging your content in your own library.

There is one final habit that will save you so much time and keep your social media running smoothly and it is super simple.

Capture Ideas As They Come To You!

Inspiration has the habit of striking at the worst of times - in the shower, driving the car, the minute your head hits the pillow – but, if you can capture your thoughts and ideas as they come to you there will rarely be a time when you are completely devoid of ideas.

As with everything we've talked about thus far, you must find a system that works for you. For me, it's simply the notes app on my phone because I always have my phone with me, and the added bonus is it syncs to all of my devices. I can capture an idea on my phone and pick it up and develop it on my laptop, it's perfect for me. Other people prefer the power of the pen and don't mind carrying a notebook with them at all times. Or you could even capture your ideas within your content library and use Trello to tie it all together. Whatever works for you!

The next step is to get into the habit of listening to those thoughts that pass through your mind throughout the day. You're probably used to listening to the biggies, like new product ideas, but it's those tiny golden nuggets that you may be overlooking or telling yourself 'I'll remember that for later' that I want you to start capturing. Sometimes it might be just a word whilst other times it might come out as a fully formed idea; even if it seems insignificant at the time get into the habit of capturing the idea in the moment and filtering it later. There's nothing worse than trying to think back to a thought you had in the middle of the night and wishing you'd written it down, and it means you'll never find yourself staring at a blank screen again.

Are You Investing Enough Time (or Too Much) into Social Media?

The other big roadblock that people hit comes down to not managing their time wisely on social media. When social media is feeling like a massive time drain that's when it becomes a problem but, the good news is, it needn't be that way.

When you're creating your social media strategy – or if you're reviewing it because you feel a little stuck – be realistic about the time you have to spend on social media. If you decide you're going to post six times a day on Facebook then be sure that you have the time and resources to do that consistently. Realistically, are you going to have time to create six high-quality posts a day, schedule them, review how they did and spend time engaging with your crowd? If the answer is no, then don't be afraid to either reduce your posting frequency or bring in some extra help to make it happen. Consistency and quality are key; don't sacrifice either for the sake of posting more.

If social media becomes too time-consuming it can start to detract from other areas of your business. As a busy business owner, social media is more than likely just one task on your mounting to-do list, and your strategy must be sustainable in order for it to be successful.

Having a strategy and a plan in place is going to go a long way towards keeping a reign on your social media marketing as, providing you refer back to it, you will be less likely to get distracted by things that aren't going to help you achieve your goals, such as wasting time on the wrong platforms. In addition to what you're going to do on social media, you may want to have some form of a plan that will guide how you manage your time. For example, it may be that you decide to create your content on specific days, schedule posts every morning and check in on comments and messages at set times throughout the day. Whatever you decide, be open to tweaking your routine as you discover what works best for you and don't be too rigid about the times when you will enter content creation mode – there's nothing like setting a time and day for inspiration to arrive to make your creativity run for the hills.

Within your routine you should also have times when you will switch off from social media. It's far too easy to end up always on duty when you don't make a conscious effort to switch off from social media –

believe me, as a social media manager this is something I have to be mindful of every single day otherwise I'd never get anything done (and I'd probably never sleep!). Make use of auto-responders on your social media pages that let people who message you know when they can expect a response. Most people are more than happy to wait providing that you set their expectations and don't leave them hanging. And remember, you don't have to go it alone so if you start getting really overwhelmed with messages on social media then consider delegating to another member of your team or outsourcing to a virtual assistant or social media manager.

Within my schedule, I also like to allow for weeks when I will switch off entirely from social media. That might sound crazy given my profession and, granted, I would love to fit in more offline weeks during the year, but I've found that it's absolutely vital to have some times when I disconnect entirely. Of course that doesn't mean that nothing goes out on social media during those times but you either need to put in some extra work beforehand to pre-schedule your posts or get some outside help to keep things ticking over whilst you take a break. It's also a good idea to have someone who can reply to messages and comments in your absence.

Be sure to allow yourself a few days at the other end to re-connect; rather than diving straight back in to creating content and scheduling posts. The whole point of taking a social media holiday is that it allows you to come back to it with a fresh pair of eyes and a renewed enthusiasm.

Bringing It All Together

Not only will your social media strategy evolve over time but so will the systems and processes you use to manage it. The key to staying on track is to be flexible but not to lose sight of your overall strategy. It's easy to get carried away by the day-to-day management of social media and before you know it you've forgotten what you were trying to achieve in the first place.

One way that you can stay on track is to treat your social media strategy as a working document. Whatever form it takes, whether a Word document, a spreadsheet, Trello board or even a stack of Post-it notes, keep referring back to it and updating it as you go along. If you update your biographies, for example, make a note in your strategy of when you did it and why. At the time it may seem insignificant, but it reminds you to check back in with your strategy so that everything you do is working towards the same goal, and it can prove surprisingly useful to be able to check back in with what you've done previously and know the rationale for doing it.

With all that in mind, I hope this has reinforced the importance of how to stay sane on social media by being conscious of how you spend your time, understanding the range of content repurposing opportunities available to you, and creating a content library that means you don't have to reinvent the wheel.

Chapter 7 – Turning Fans Into Paying Customers

Why is nobody buying?

Once you have begun attracting some engagement on social media, your thoughts will naturally turn to that 'what next' question – how do I actually get people to buy? Why is nobody biting?

If you are just starting out on social media and you're using this book to create a strategy that will guide you as your presence grows, then you are already a step ahead. The sooner you consider how your fans will eventually become paying customers the better, but if you've been using social media as a business for a while then don't despair; it's never too late to turn things around.

First off, do your followers know what you have on offer? Or are your paid offerings your best kept secret?

It may sound obvious but if you're a stealth seller then chances are no-one actually knows what they can buy from you. For soulful entrepreneurs, selling can feel icky. We worry that people will get annoyed if we start pushing our paid products or services, or fed up if we mention them too often. But the truth is, if you're not letting your crowd know how they can work with you then you're doing them a disservice; you're denying them the opportunity to get the help and support that they truly need from you. There will be people who hit the unlike button as soon as you start sharing a paid product or service but, in all honesty, those people were never going to buy from you anyway. They are not your ideal clients and it's a good way to filter them out because it brings you a step closer to helping the people who really need what you have to offer.

That being said, if you are overly promotional in your social media posts then you might start deterring your ideal clients. What a minefield! How on earth do you strike the balance between presenting valuable opportunities and not being seen as spam?

Unfortunately, there's no fixed guideline here, but if you're looking for a benchmark then an 80 / 20 split (80% non-sales and value-added content and 20% promotional) is a good starting point. As with all aspects of social media marketing, what works for your business may not necessarily work for another. Once you start promoting it's all about testing what works for your business and your crowd.

On Facebook, in particular, you will find that as soon as you share promotional posts your organic reach takes a hit. Facebook is extremely sophisticated in the way that it can understand what your posts are about and it will show less promotional posts in the Newsfeed than other types of post; potentially because they would prefer you to spend advertising budget on getting eyes on your offerings. You may also find that promotional posts get less engagement.

When it comes to promotional posts, as well as looking at reach and engagement, it's wise to keep an eye on the number of unfollows you receive, in addition to the 'hide post', 'hide all posts' and 'mark as spam' options on Facebook. As I said, some people will unfollow and that's OK. Likewise, those followers who aren't actually interested in paying to work with you or buy your product may hide or unfollow your posts; some may even mark them as spam. A small amount of this activity is not something to panic over but if you notice that it's increasing then that may be a signal to ease back on the promotion and re-assess your balance of content.

Overcoming Barriers and Objections

In Chapter 2, we touched on the barriers and objections that might hold your followers back from making a purchase. This is one of the most common reasons you may find it a struggle to convert fans into paying customers so let's explore it in more depth.

Perhaps you have fans who have followed you for a while and begun to engage, and yet they aren't taking that final step to becoming a paying customer. Why not?

The first purchase from a customer is often the hardest to secure because they don't yet know what it's like to work with you or they aren't wholly convinced of the outcomes you can deliver. Some people will contact you directly to obtain answers to their questions and the aspects of your service that they're unsure about, but many won't.

The beauty of social media is that it gives you an opportunity to tackle common objections and barriers head on. If you can answer someone's question or concern before they even have to ask it not only can you accelerate their journey to becoming a customer but your customers are likely to be happier and more loyal from the outset because they were convinced of your offering before they purchased. Customers who complain are often the ones who didn't really understand what they were getting into in the first place. Wouldn't it be great if you could avoid this and get more sales?

Start by making a list of all the concerns that might be holding your followers back. Common barriers include:

- They don't (yet) see the value in what you offer which makes it seem too expensive.

- Often #1 is because they don't fully understand what you're offering and they're unaware of the outcomes they'll see as a result of your product or service.
- They've had a bad experience with a business or person who offers a similar product or service to you and this has created trust issues; they're wary of being let down again and / or wasting money.
- If you provide a service, they don't know enough about you to know whether you're a good fit for them.
- They don't value themselves and / or their business enough to invest in it.

There are many more potential barriers, including those that are unique to your business, and you will learn more as you tune into the conversations you have with your crowd.

Looking over your list may feel overwhelming at first. How on earth can you tackle these their concerns without talking to each potential customer individually?

The first thing to know is that if you're addressing objections head on then often people will feel more comfortable to get in touch if they are sitting on the fence and need a more information or reassurance. Meanwhile, for some potential customers, and depending on how much you are asking people to spend, seeing the answer to their question on social media, without even having to ask, will be enough to convince them.

Using Content to Nurture Your Followers

Within the list of objections that you've created, there will be stacks of ideas for social media posts, not to mention blog posts, emails and content for your website. The work we did in Chapter 5 will hopefully have inspired plentiful ideas for the content that you could create. When you address your ideal client's struggles and desires in your social media content, you may find yourself touching on objections and their unasked questions. However, you should also consider creating content specifically around the list of barriers that you've just created, in order to reinforce your message, nurture leads and remove unnecessary uncertainty.

If you know that it is likely they've had a bad experience with purchasing a similar product or service from another business in the past, think about how you could address that in a post. For example, 'I know that you may have been let down in the past because of XYZ' or 'I know that XYZ problem is rife in this industry, but this is why my business is different'.

If you feel that your followers may not understand exactly what you're offering, could you collect together some of your most frequently asked questions and answer them on social media?

Show, Don't Tell

There is a myriad of possibilities, which will vary depending on the barriers you're tackling, but a good guideline is to always show, rather than tell.

You could talk all day about how great your product or service is, why they won't be disappointed and how it's different to anything they've experienced before, but why should they believe you? As marketers we're naturally going to rave about our own offering. If you can demonstrably show the value of your offering, rather than simply telling, it will be much more convincing.

Testimonials, reviews and case studies are invaluable in this respect as they provide social proof. In other words, if someone in a similar position as yourself tells you how amazing something is then you are much more likely to believe them than if the person selling the product or service tells you the same.

Be aware, however, that there is a lot of scepticism around testimonials. It's no longer enough to simply share good feedback from a client as people may question whether it is actually genuine. You must consider how you can add credibility to your testimonials. This can be as simple as tagging the customer who provided the testimonial in your post, providing some background information to the testimonial or opting for video testimonials over written, if your customers are willing.

Case studies go beyond the box standard testimonial and can address many more of the objections your potential customers may have. They tend to give more insight into what it's like to work with you and how the process flows from beginning to end. If you can illustrate what to expect from their very first enquiry to the moment your product or service is delivered and the outcomes that are delivered it will go a long way towards putting potential customers at ease.

I know that for many soulful entrepreneurs, sharing testimonials and even case studies can carry the ick factor. You may be afraid of showboating and don't want people to get the sense that all you do is shout about how amazing you are. It is all about finding a way to share this type of content that feels authentic to you.

If you do start to feel uneasy around sharing testimonials, refer back to your strategy to remind you of the purpose that they serve. This is not about peacocking; it's about helping your crowd to make an informed decision that they won't regret. In that way, you are doing them a service; we've all experienced the disappointment of making an impulse purchase only to find yourself feeling let down and questioning what the hell you were thinking!

What's more, whilst testimonials and case studies have a role to play, they are not the only way that you can show rather than tell.

Think back to the lessons you have learned, whether it be in business or in life. Did you have a negative experience that made you commit to doing business a different way? Or perhaps you notice on something in your day-to-day life, such as a poor customer service experience, which you can then share as an anecdote. Just bear in mind, this is about pulling the lessons out of life, not naming and shaming other businesses.

Bringing It All Together

If it seems like there is a lot to take in, then please don't panic. As with everything in this book, this is about setting you off on your journey and providing you with a touch point to check back in with whenever you find yourself stuck or off track.

Over time you will learn a great deal more about your crowd, their expectations, and the reservations that may hold them back from purchasing from you. This is where your ideal client journal will be especially useful as it gives you a central place to record everything you learn about your crowd over time.

Don't be afraid to make a note of unanswered questions as well. If you find yourself struggling to pinpoint why potential customers might be uncertain about buying from you then make a note of it and set yourself an action to find out.

Also, be mindful that your content strategy will evolve over time. To begin with, testimonials and frequently asked questions (FAQs) may seem the obvious route to take, but as you become more familiar with your crowd you will, no doubt, find more ways to weave your message into other types of content as well.

Heading into the next chapter, we are going to take everything you've learnt so far and look at the ways that you can continue improving and making progress on social media from this point on.

Chapter 8 - When is it Time to Up-Level?

As your presence on social media grows, there will be times when you feel ready to take things to the next level. I call this up-levelling and it is the process of evolving your strategy.

You have reached the point where you have a solid foundation in place, you have an engaged crowd and you are posting consistently. That's not to say that your crowd is huge or that you're posting vast amounts of content; the keywords here are engaged and consistent.

You will reach this point more than once.

When you first start out on social media, you will be focused on setting up your platforms, building a small audience and learning what to post on your pages. At the point where you're comfortable with this you are ready to up-level.

That means reflecting on how things are going so far - what's working well, what's not working so well? Where are you using your time efficiently? Where does it feel like your time is being drained or wasted?

The important question to ask is - what can I do now to build on my foundation and make things grow? That growth could include;

- Followers
- Engagement on your posts
- Organic reach
- Direct sales
- Traffic to your website

What growth looks like for your business will depend on your goals. So knowing what you want to achieve from social media is essential for you to be able to plot the steps you will take to move to the next level.

Where Are You Focusing Your Efforts?

Choosing which social media platforms to focus your efforts on is not a one-off decision. Not only is social media evolving on a daily basis but your crowd and their habits will evolve over time as well. It's important that you regularly review which platforms you're using, how effectively you are using them and whether there are any additional places you should be placing your attention. If you overlook this step then you may come to find that you have spent time and resources in the wrong places and overlooked other opportunities, so it really is important.

One thing to keep in mind as you enter this process is that the return on investment from every social media platform you use won't necessarily be monetary. On some platforms you may find that you can generate direct sales but on others, the return on investment may include increased brand awareness, PR opportunities secured, more traffic to your website, subscribers added to your email list, and the list goes on.

As you review the social media platforms that you're using, ask yourself;

- What is my purpose on this platform?
- How does that purpose fit into my overall marketing strategy and business objectives?
- Am I using this platform to its full potential? Or are there elements that I need to learn more about or invest more time / money / resources into?
- Am I being creative enough and standing out or is my content blending in with the masses?

- Am I wasting time on this platform and, if so, how could my process be made more efficient? Is there a tool I could use to streamline this process or do I need to consider delegating?

Answering these questions will light your path and give you a clear direction to follow in order to progress your strategy.

Are There Any Platforms You're Ignoring or Avoiding?

In the early stages of creating your social media strategy it's OK to concentrate on one or two platforms based on where you feel most comfortable, as well as, of course, where your ideal clients are hanging out. It takes time to build a social media strategy and trying to be everywhere at once in the early days will likely result in you spreading your resources too thin and getting mediocre results all round.

Having said that, as you progress with your strategy and you have your primary platforms running smoothly, it may be time to branch out by reassessing platforms that you may have previously ignored or outright avoided.

This is still not to say that you should try to be everywhere all at once, but you should carry out an objective appraisal of your strategy and address whether there are any platforms that could benefit your business but which you are not currently utilising.

If that's the case but you're not sure where to start or how to use a platform to its full potential, then ask for help. You can save yourself a great deal of time and avoid making mistakes by getting outside help, such as training or coaching, and it can also remove any temptation to procrastinate by holding you accountable.

What Are The Numbers Telling You?

'Marketing without data is like driving with your eyes closed.' – Dan Zarella

The more you look at the analytics data built into your social media accounts the more insight you will have to guide the development of your strategy.

If you can do this on a monthly basis, or work with a social media professional who can handle the data for you, then that would be the ideal. But, as a minimum you should look at your analytics each time you review and up-level your strategy.

A good starting point is to make a note of the numbers at the beginning of every month as this will allow you to see, in broad brush strokes, how things are progressing. Initially, you can focus on the headline stats – number of followers, overall reach, engagement, organic reach vs paid reach and clicks on posts. The important thing is not to look at these stats purely as achievements. The truth is, it doesn't really matter if you have 100 or 100,000 followers, the questions you should be asking are:

- Am I attracting the right people?
- Am I gaining new followers or have my accounts plateaued?
- Are my followers engaging with my posts?
- Are my followers converting into paying customers?

There's a lot of insight you can glean from these headline stats but the more you dig into the data, the more detail you will be able to add to your map. If numbers and spreadsheets bring you out in cold sweats then you don't have to avoid it and you definitely shouldn't; instead, ask someone who knows what they're doing to help and advise you. You will then be able to start asking more meaningful questions such as:

- What post format gets the best reach / engagement?
- What type of content gets the best reach / engagement?
- How can I create more shareable content?
- Are long or short videos working best right not?
- Which perform best, pre-recorded or live videos?

Of course, the whole exercise is only going to benefit your business if you follow it through and take action. So, once you've gathered the insight into what is working, and therefore what you should be doing more of, and where there are areas of improvement, create an action plan. This can take any form as long as it's not going to be filed away and forgotten about. It could be a simple tick list, a Trello board, a spreadsheet or even a bunch of Post-it notes stuck to your office wall.

Growing Pains Are A Positive Sign

You may feel the temptation to stay within your comfort zone and yes, once you've found your rhythm on social media it becomes easier to manage and be consistent with, but it can also begin to feel stale. Your followers may start to feel like they've seen it all before. At best they start overlooking some of your posts and at worse they hit the unfollow button.

Your challenge now is to keep innovating and trying new things - without throwing the baby out with the bathwater!

Not only will you keep your followers interested and engaged, you will also future-proof your strategy because you're not relying too heavily on one tactic or formula that could be thrown into disarray by a sudden algorithm change.

Each time you step your social media strategy up a gear you may well find that things become harder for a time. You will probably find yourself investing more time into your social media marketing and things will fall into your path that you're not sure how to deal with (yet).

These are simply growing pains and they are positive. They mean that you are challenging yourself and pushing your business into new territories. If you shy away from up-levelling and stay stuck within your comfort zone then your social media will eventually stagnate. Your crowd won't grow, which means that you will be selling to the same people all of the time so, at best, the potential for your business to grow is limited and at worst it risks sales drying up.

The good news is that over time you will become comfortable with your strategy again, you'll enjoy a period of consolidating everything you've put into place until you reach the point where you need to up-level once again.

You Don't Have To Go It Alone, In Fact, You Really Mustn't

Now this may sound a little backwards, but the more you advance your social media strategy the more you will find yourself needing to ask for help.

Take this example, when you first start out on social media you might be unsure how to set up a Twitter account. It's relatively easy to find this information out through a quick Google search, a glance at Twitter's help centre or by watching a few YouTube videos. Once you have everything set up, you'll turn your attention to content and you'll probably be looking for top tips – there will be lots of quick wins at this early stage. You can find stacks of information online to help you with this in the form of blogs, articles, social media, books and videos.

As you become more advanced the help that you need is more than just tips, tricks and how-tos. It becomes much more individual to your business. Those tips and tricks that you relied on in the beginning will only take you so far, the next step is to truly understand what's working for your business on social media at any given time and how to use that insight to move your strategy forward.

I absolutely encourage you to start getting to grips with the analytics that are built into your social media accounts but don't underestimate the value of having a second pair of eyes on your strategy as well.

A second pair of eyes isn't a substitute for keeping your own finger on the pulse, but it will help you to progress faster. A second pair of eyes on any element of your business is valuable because it means a fresh perspective, new ideas and a critical eye.

More than that, looking at analytics data to measure progress is one thing but knowing how it fits into wider trends and what to do with the insight you gather is another. Building a partnership with a social media professional who has their finger on the pulse of social media trends and is experienced in social media analytics and strategy building will allow your business to grow faster, give you the peace of mind that you're not missing out or making costly mistakes, and free up your time to focus on other areas of your business.

Bringing It All Together

You now know how to craft a soulful social media strategy for your business, from choosing the right platforms to creating content, putting your strategy to the test and using analytics to improve and up-level your marketing. In the final chapter I'm going to prepare you to set off on your journey into the world of social media with a fresh approach and a renewed gusto. We'll also talk about staying on track and the importance of learning to trust your gut as you navigate around social media.

As You Embark On Your Journey...

When you first start out on social media or you're creating a strategy for the first time, you will no doubt be brimming with enthusiasm. Social media is placed firmly on your list of priorities at this point - if it wasn't then you probably wouldn't have picked up this book in the first place.

However, it's easy for that enthusiasm to wane and I've seen how this happens time and time again. As I've said throughout this book, social media marketing is a marathon not a race. In fact, it's a marathon with no actual finish line so it's no surprise that you may get tired. Hopefully the strategies I've shared with you are going to help to keep you energised and enthused but there's one final reminder I want to leave you with.

Social media must remain on your priority list for it to add value to your business.

I know how busy you are running your business and how many plates you have to keep spinning every day, but the minute that marketing becomes one of those ‘I’ll do it when I have time’ or ‘I’ll pop something on Facebook when I get a minute’ is the time when your business will begin to stagnate. It won’t happen straightaway. In fact, you may not even notice until it’s too late. But the time to market is when you’re busy, not when things go quiet and you’re desperate for business.

Small steps taken consistently every day will keep you moving forward.

There's a quote from Laura Vanderkam, author of *What the Most Successful People Do Before Breakfast*, that I love and which serves to remind us of the choice we have when it comes to our time.

'Instead of saying "I don't have time" try saying "it's not a priority" and see how that feels.' Laura then goes on to explain; 'Changing our language reminds us that time is a choice. If we don't like how we're spending an hour, we can choose differently.'

So, if ever you find yourself saying you don't have time for social media, I want you to ask yourself whether social media is a priority for your business. Can you afford not to be on social media and using it effectively to reach your ideal clients and attract new business?

Take Time To Acknowledge How Far You've Come

It's easy to lose sight of where you started and how far you've come, not only on social media but in every aspect of your business. Not taking time to look back and acknowledge your progress is a sure-fire way to end up feeling disheartened when you're looking ahead to all that you still want to achieve.

Bear in mind that your idea of what success looks like will change and evolve over time. Each time you approach 'success' you will naturally move the goal posts as your view expands and you set new goals. So, when you go through the up-levelling process we talked about in Chapter 8 and you're taking time out to review your social media, remember that it's not only about identifying the areas where you can improve. When I'm working with clients 1-2-1 we always spend some time looking at what is already working really well and where they have made progress and improvements. And that's not just about keeping motivation high.

In fact, sometimes you can learn as much from what is working well as you can from looking at the areas which you'd like to improve.

Be Willing to Adapt and Evolve

It's not just about being slow and steady to win the race. There will be times when you need to speed up and other times when you may even need to change direction. Working through this book and reviewing your strategy regularly is only going to be of value to your business if you are willing to be flexible, to adapt and to evolve as time goes by.

Social media is, of course, always changing and it has reached the point where there seems to be a new feature, tool and even new platforms being released on a daily basis. How on earth can you stay on top of it all and not get left behind?

The key is to stay aligned with your strategy and avoid bright, shiny object syndrome. When you hear about something new, it's tempting to think you need to jump on it right away, whether that's out of excitement or the fear of missing an opportunity.

Instead, before you take any action, I want you to check back in with your social media strategy and ask yourself the following questions:

- Will using it help me to reach my ideal clients?
- Is this new feature / tool / platform going to help me get closer to achieving my goals?
- Is it the best use of my time right now?
- Is it going to distract or detract from other important elements of my strategy?

You can also run any new ideas that come to mind through this same filter.

If that thing you are thinking of doing is going to help you reach your ideal clients, get closer to achieving your goals and you have the time, energy and resources to use it effectively without detracting from anything else you're doing on social media, then consider taking it forward.

It's tempting to jump straight in and there is certainly a time for reacting quickly and getting ahead of the curve but taking even just an hour to work that new thing into your existing strategy will pay dividends in the long run. It will give you a direction to follow and ensure that all of your efforts are working effectively together.

The other area that you need to be ready and willing to adapt is in relation to your ideal clients. Your crowd will evolve over time, both in terms of their wants and needs and in terms of your understanding of them. The more you seek to learn about your crowd, the more effective your marketing will be as you will become adept at crafting and presenting to them the right message at the right time. But learning about their struggles and their desires is only worthwhile if you are going to use that information to inform your strategy. In Chapter 2, I suggested that you keep an ideal client journal to keep a rolling record of all the things you learn about your crowd. In addition to that, schedule time in your diary to review what you've noted in your journal, as there may be quick notes and musings that need to be fed back into your social media strategy. To reiterate, this doesn't have to be a laborious task and it isn't about creating a lengthy document only for it to be filed away and forgotten about. Find a system that works for you, even if it takes a little trial and error to master it.

Become Your Own Guiding Light

Perhaps the biggest stumbling block you might encounter on your social media journey is the wealth of information and advice that is so readily accessible. What begins as a blessing can become a source of confusion and overwhelm, as you find yourself presented with so many varying opinions from many different sources.

My hope is for this book to empower you to take ownership of your business's social media strategy. By working through the steps in this book, you will create a strategy that fits with your business. You will not be blindly following someone else's strategy on the basis that it is working for them or their clients, but following your own, bespoke strategy that fits perfectly with your own ethos and mission.

That doesn't mean to say you ignore outside advice, there is always something more that we can learn after all, but that you embed the filter I talked about above into your way of thinking. When you hear of a new strategy or tactic that everyone seems to be raving about, you now have a filter to run it through which will tell you whether it is worth investing your time and resources into. It may not come easily at first but as you progress it will become a natural process and your gut will begin to tell you if something is right for your business or not.

Our Journey Doesn't End Here

I truly hope that you have enjoyed reading this book and it has left you feeling enthused and empowered to create a social media strategy that is oozing with integrity and soul and which will, ultimately, help you achieve your business dreams.

The good news is that this is just the start of our journey together! Flick to the Connect with the Author Page where you will find the best ways to connect with me, keep in touch and stay up to date with the latest developments in the world of social media.

I've also prepared a stack of bonus resources which you can go ahead and grab by popping over to **http://www.infinity-digital.co.uk/social-media-handbook-bonus-resources**. If you'd like to receive the latest social media news and even more support for your strategy then you can also sign up to my weekly newsletter over on the bonus resources page.

Dedication

For all you soulful entrepreneurs that have picked up this book I want to say thank you from the bottom of my heart. For as long as I can remember, it has been a dream of mine to write a book. I was waiting for the right moment, the right time to share my message and this is it. I am truly passionate about helping other people to achieve their dreams of starting their own business. I've seen, first-hand, the power that social media has to help us achieve those dreams, not only of starting a business but of building it into something that we adore and that supports us in every aspect of our lives. I hope that this book has inspired you and equipped you with some of the tools you need to make that dream a reality.

I want to say a big, big thank you to everyone who has helped me on my business journey and worked with me to create the book that you are holding in your hands today. I could not have done this without the help and support of my amazing editor and writing mentor Michelle Emerson, the incredibly talented Vicki Nicolson who created the book cover and my wonderful assistant Claire Bourke who keeps me organised and accountable every single day. A special thanks also goes to Emma Holmes for believing in me when I didn't believe in myself and inspiring me to show up, be myself and share my message each and every day.

And to my family - you are my rocks! Every one of you has encouraged me to shoot for the stars and chase my dreams right from day one. Even in the early days when I'm pretty sure everyone thought I was just messing around on Facebook(!), you had faith in me and supported me every step of the way. To Dylan for always making me smile, being wise beyond your years and altogether unimpressed no matter how many people view my YouTube videos! And to my husband, James, for your unwavering support, belief in me and for being infinitely patient when I'm chewing your ear off with business ideas or boring you with my incessant talk of algorithms and engagement.

As they say, it takes a village, and this book, not to mention my business, would not be a reality without every single person who has supported me along the way.

Connect with the Author

Feel free to pop by my website and also connect with me on social media, where you'll see my tips, advice, and strategies being put to good use.

- https://www.facebook.com/InfinitywithBeckieCoupe
- https://twitter.com/rebeccacoupe
- https://www.youtube.com/channel/UCaUJxGfM6k838Oh712PMkKQ
- https://www.instagram.com/rebeccacoupe/
- https://www.pinterest.co.uk/InfinityDigi
- http://infinity-digital.co.uk

And here's the link to those bonuses I've been telling you about:

http://infinity-digital.co.uk/social-media-handbook-bonus-resources

About the Author

Having worked with social media since the early days of Facebook and Twitter way back in 2007, Beckie took the leap in 2014 and founded Infinity. Her mission? To help those with a dream of being in business make that their reality by harnessing the power of social media.

She's worked with hundreds of business owners to give them the confidence to use social media and truly make it their own. To show up, stand out and shine online. To shout their message from the rooftops, attract their dream clients and create a business and a lifestyle that they adore!

Printed in Great Britain
by Amazon